Ethnicity and Development

Ethnicity and Development explores the impact of ethnic fragmentation on the success or failure of nations and uses case studies of Bangladesh and Pakistan to illustrate this. It analyzes the role of institutions in engendering economic and social progress and challenges the New Institutional Economics (NIE) narrative.

The book argues that the NIE narrative has some gaps, particularly that it is blind to ethnic fragmentation and therefore does not account for the construction of institutions that can build national cohesion in low- and low-middle-income countries (L/LMICs). It shows that L/LMICs have a different cultural context and that they need to first build national cohesion on a foundation of horizontal – across ethnic groups – and vertical – across classes – equity. The author's analysis also examines other novel issues, such as the boost that is provided by nations acquiring the right of self-determination. Other novelties are the distinction between prime causes (triggers) for economic development and approaches for economic development. More important for this book is the distinction between natural and constructed nations and the conceptual framework presented to analyze their performance. Finally, the study examines the creation of national cohesion in ethnically diverse nations.

Addressing a gap in the literature, this book will be of interest to researchers in development economics, political science and sociology and specialists in comparative politics/political theory with a focus on Area Studies.

Shahrukh Rafi Khan is currently a research associate at Mount Holyoke College, South Hadley, Massachusetts. He has published extensively in refereed journals and authored and edited numerous books. His recent books include *Economic Successes in South Asia: A Story of Partnerships* (Routledge, 2022); *Spontaneous and Induced Collective Action in Pakistani Rural Development* (with Shaheen Rafi Khan, Palgrave Macmillan, 2021); *Development Economics: A Critical Introduction* (Routledge, 2020); *A Microcredit Alternative in South Asia* (with Natasha Ansari, Routledge, 2018); *Routledge History of Development Economics Thought* (Routledge, 2014); and *Market as Means Not Master: Towards New Developmentalism* (Routledge, 2010).

Routledge Studies in the Growth Economies of Asia

Ethnicity and Development

Addressing the Gaps in New
Institutional Economics

Shahrukh Rafi Khan

Routledge
Taylor & Francis Group
LONDON AND NEW YORK

First published 2024
by Routledge
4 Park Square, Milton Park, Abingdon, Oxon OX14 4RN

and by Routledge
605 Third Avenue, New York, NY 10158

Routledge is an imprint of the Taylor & Francis Group, an informa business

British Library Cataloguing-in-Publication Data
A catalogue record for this book is available from the British Library

ISBN: 978-1-032-63082-3 (hbk)
ISBN: 978-1-032-63083-0 (pbk)
ISBN: 978-1-032-63087-8 (ebk)

DOI: 10.4324/9781032630878

Typeset in Times New Roman
by Apex CoVantage, LLC

For Stephanie Bunker

Contents

Tables

Preface

I have been working in the development economics field since 1973 when I joined the Pakistan Institute of Development Economics (PIDE) as a research economist with a bachelor's degree from the London School of Economics (LSE). While a student at the LSE, I imbibed, based on self-study, the political philosophy of the right of nations to self-determination. This belief was tested when East Pakistan engaged in a struggle for independence against West Pakistan.

East Pakistani economists working in PIDE, then based in Dhaka,[1] had shown how West Pakistan was draining resources from East Pakistan by not providing its due share, based on the National Finance Commission awards, and essentially arresting its economic growth and development.[2] Pakistan wisely adopted a quota system in 1948, one year after its independence, to give greater representation, in, for example, the civil service and universities, to the less developed regions. However, East Pakistan got only a 42 percent quota,[3] even though it had 57 percent of the population.[4]

When economic exploitation and underrepresentation in key national organizations merged with political high-handedness, the East Pakistanis revolted and sought an independent state. The political high-handedness, which proved to be the tipping point in the tolerance of the East Pakistanis, was the refusal to concede legitimate political power to an East Pakistani politician (Sheikh Mujibur-Rahman) by the Pakistani dictator, General Yahya Khan, in cahoots with the West Pakistani politician Zulfiqar Ali Bhutto. The latter had won the popular vote in West Pakistan, but East Pakistan, at the time of this political crisis, in 1971, had a larger population and vote bank.

As a West Pakistani student in London, following the political philosophy I believed to be correct on this issue, I supported East Pakistan's right to self-determination. The atrocities committed by the West Pakistani military[5] cemented my support for the East Pakistani cause. With the assistance of the Indian military, the difficult terrain, the incompetence and of the West Pakistan army fighting a thousand miles away from home, and the determination of the *Mukti Bahini* fighting for a homeland, East Pakistan succeeded in its war of liberation. In 1971, Bangladesh became the world's newest nation-state.

The Bangladeshi struggle had a big impact on me, particularly since I differed from many of my West Pakistani friends in supporting its cause. After Bangladesh attained independence, most of my Pakistani friends and colleagues viewed Bangladesh as a lost cause well into the twenty-first century. Reviewing the data, I noted with fascination how well the country was progressing on the social and economic fronts. While in 1971 all social and economic indicators for Bangladesh trailed way behind Pakistan, by 2021, a mere five decades later, Bangladesh dominated Pakistan in all social and economic indicators (Chapter 3).

As a scholar from a low-income country (LIC), now a low-middle-income country (LMIC), I have been concerned with catch-up growth all my academic life.[6] In my textbook on development economics (Khan, 2020), the concluding chapter speculated about triggers for catch-up growth. This book has emerged as a continuation of that speculation and argues that national cohesion, which could result from ethnic commonality, could be one such trigger.[7] Another could be the morale boost brought about by independence itself. I reached this conclusion in observing Bangladesh's economic acceleration contrasted with Pakistan's corresponding stall at the turn of the twenty-first century. Bangladesh has one major ethnic group (98 percent Bengali), while Pakistan has six notable ethnic groups, with the Punjabis predominant at 45 percent.[8]

While this book is devoted to the study of nations, personally I would prefer to live in a world without nations and borders.[9] Of course, this is not likely to happen for centuries, if at all. Currently there is little sign that the world is moving toward a borderless world, other than deference to some extent to the United Nations' coordination on the related global challenges of climate change and biodiversity and pandemics. Other positive signs are the elimination of borders in Europe and the growth of African consciousness.

Perhaps humanity's common struggle against the climate disaster may eventually help the world to inch in the direction of world consciousness, but it is clear that for now nation-states are a political reality, and many, unfortunately, are dealing with a bad hand, in that they are not *natural* nations but rather colonial constructs. A natural nation is arbitrarily defined as a nation within a defined geographic space where the dominant ethnicity is 90 percent or more of the population.

The distinction between natural and constructed nations as a central feature of this book is elaborated on in Chapter 2. This distinction also plays into the main research question explored in this book, that is, what if any role does this distinction between natural and constructed nations play in explaining the success of nations.

Explaining the success or failure of nations is an important genre in the literature going back to Adam Smith and before. One successful explanation pertains to the role of institutions in New Institutional Economics (NIE). This book explores an institutional explanation as a prime cause for catch-up growth and suggest that, as an economic development story, it has some gaps in that it is blind to ethnic fragmentation and does not account for the construction of institutions that can build national cohesion in L/LMICs. NIE explores the evolution of institutions in HICs (rule of law, property rights, contract enforcement) that facilitated market-based transactions and that culture and path dependency played a considerable role in this process. This book argues that L/LMICs have a different cultural context and that they need to build national cohesion on a foundation of horizontal (across ethnic groups) and vertical (across classes) equity.

National cohesion and how it could come about in ethnically fragmented nations is proffered as a complement to the NIE story. A distinction is made in this book between a prime cause, a trigger for development and approaches for economic development such as developmentalism or neo-liberalism. National cohesion is posited as a prime cause for ethnically fragmented nations within the broad rubric of the NIE story.

Chapter 1 explores the thinking of key contributors to the NIE narrative. It identifies the key gaps in this narrative that are addressed in the rest of the book. Chapter 2 elaborates on the distinction between natural and constructed nations and provides a conceptual framework to analyze their performance in terms of social and economic development. The methodology section indicates how data were collected and used to provide evidence pertaining to the research question in this book: how the status of being a natural or constructed nation impacts social and economic performance.

Chapter 3 explores the incidence of ethnicity and ethnic conflict in low- and middle-income countries following from the hypothesis that ethnic diversity in constructed nations results in conflict and undermines national cohesion. The literature on ethnicity and economic development is reviewed next to explore if and the extent to which diverse ethnicities in constructed nations undermine economic growth and development.

Chapter 4 focuses on two related stories. The overarching story is of independence of nations in a changed geography. The contention is that the morale boost and national drive that is likely to accompany independence can enhance economic and social development. The related story is that of ethnic homogeneity and how that might enhance economic development. This chapter first considers a comparative case study, which comes close to a natural experiment, of Bangladesh and Pakistan and documents Bangladesh's remarkable social and economic success. Since independence, per se, might have provided an additional boost to social and economic progress, this hypothesis is explored next.

The Balkan nations, born after the collapse of the Soviet Union, varied in terms of ethnic cohesion. Only half of the eight Balkan countries that declared independence after the collapse of the Soviet Union could be considered natural nations (with a dominant ethnicity of about 90 percent or more). This provided the opportunity to explore the impact of independence even if it was not accompanied by the national cohesion that might accompany being a natural nation.

Chapter 5 focuses on how constructed nations, mostly a colonial legacy, can create national cohesion and in this regard simulate the success of natural nations. While there has been much research on the negative association of ethnic diversity with conflict and economic growth, there has been much less focus on building national cohesion. Chapter 5 first delineates some of the common strategies used for engendering national cohesion. Next it presents case studies of noted successes in creating national cohesion. It also reviews Pakistan's struggle with handling ethnic separatism in Balochistan, one of its four provinces. The latter case study shows how Pakistan mishandled this ethnic conflict and also some promising strategies subsequently employed to build national cohesion.

There are several novelties in the book not covered elsewhere. The focus on the boost that is provided by nations acquiring the right of self-determination has not, to the author's knowledge, been covered in the literature. This, of course, has far-reaching implications when global policy makers are considering the fate of natural nations seeking self-determination. Other novelties are the distinction between prime causes (triggers) for economic development and approaches for economic development. More important for this book is the distinction between natural and constructed nations and the conceptual framework presented to analyze their performance. Finally, much of the literature focuses on the negative impact of ethnic diversity on economic growth and development, but there is much less attention paid to creating national cohesion in ethnically diverse nations. The book seeks to address this shortcoming.

I would like to thank Shaheen Rafi Khan for reading the draft manuscript and providing many valuable comments and suggestions. I have much to thank the reviewers of this book for their criticisms and guidance that have, I think, resulted in a restructured and improved book.

Many thanks are due to Dorothea Schaefter, Senior Editor of Asian Studies for Routledge, for her encouragement, for overseeing a rigorous review process and for providing helpful advice when called for at all stages in writing the book, from proposal preparation to manuscript completion. Also, many thanks are due to Saraswathy Narayan for efficiently and competently preparing the manuscript for handover to the production department.

Finally, thanks are due to Mount Holyoke College for their research support.

Notes

1 PIDE moved to West Pakistan after Bangladesh declared independence, and Bangladesh Institute of Development Studies was formed in its stead as a new nation.
2 For example, Bangladeshi economists argued that jute from East Pakistan was Pakistan's main foreign currency earner and that this was used for industrialization in

West Pakistan, which, in turn, used East Pakistan as a market for consumer goods. While western scholars were persuaded by this analysis, refer to Burki (1972) for a dissenting view. He conceded that West Pakistan ran a trade surplus with East Pakistan, but argued that there was a net transfer of resources from West to East Pakistan. Tax incentives resulted in the move of West Pakistani capital to East Pakistan, and while East Pakistan contributed less than a third of central government revenue, it was allocated more than 50 percent of this revenue. In all, he estimated that these transfers to East Pakistan from West Pakistan amounted to 2.3 percent of the latter's gross domestic product (GDP).

3 While East Pakistan's quota in the civil service was 42 percent versus its population share of 57 percent, this quota was in place only for one year, 1948, before it was replaced with a provincial quota of 40 percent for East Pakistan with 20 percent reserved for open merit (https://en.wikipedia.org/wiki/Quota_system_in_Pakistan, consulted December 5, 2022). In effect this further disenfranchised East Pakistanis since the number of college graduates was far higher in the West than in the East (www.dawn.com/news/753508/east-wing-beats-west-wing-in-literacy-rate, consulted December 5, 2022).

4 Abdul Wajid Rana, "Quota system in Pakistan", *The Express Tribune*, November 9, 2017, https://tribune.com.pk/story/1553353/6-quota-system-pakistan, consulted May 25, 2022. The gross underrepresentation of East Pakistan in the civil service and military has been documented by Jahan (1972). For example, Bengalis in the military officer class in the army, navy and air force had 1.5, 1.2 and 8.6 percent representation, respectively. They had zero percent representation at the highest tier of the civil service (secretary) and less than 8 percent at the officer ranks below that.

5 To be fair, atrocities were committed by *Mukti Bahini* also, the vanguard force of the liberation struggle, including against civilians of a different ethnicity (Biharis) deemed to be or actually supporting West Pakistan. Atrocities committed by both sides of the war are well documented, but there is a distinction between the actions of an occupying army and those of the vanguard of a population fighting for liberation.

6 "Catch-up" is defined as the economic process that some low- and low-middle-income countries (L/LMIC) undergo to converge to the per capita income levels of high-income countries (HIC). Catch-up or convergence occurs if high economic growth is sustained for several decades because it can lead to a several-fold doubling of per capita GDP. Compounding and "the rule of 72" explain this. Take the growth rate of any variable, in this case the per capita gross domestic product (PCGDP), and divide it into 72, and this explains how long it would take the variable to double. Thus, if the per capita GDP is growing at 7 percent, it doubles in about ten years. If it grows at an average of 10 percent, it takes only about seven years for the doubling. This is how convergence to the income level of HICs can happen due to catch-up growth in economies that start with a low base.

7 Ideology could generate national cohesion, at least in the short to medium terms, if prosperity is delivered such as in China. While religion could play a similar role, as was initially the case after the Islamic revolution of 1978–1979 in Iran, the centralizing tendency of the Shia sect and the inability to deliver sustained prosperity, partly due to western hostility, created disaffection. Even so, religious commonality could, in principle, create cohesion, but, to do so, it would require the absence of sectarian diversity. Sectarian conflict, as in the case of Pakistan and Afghanistan, is a major challenge for national cohesion.

8 Data on national ethnicity are drawn from www.nationmaster.com/country-info/stats/People/Ethnic-groups, consulted February 23, 2022.

9 John Lennon's line, "imagine there's no countries", in his popular song "Imagine" is inspirational.

References

Burki, S.J. 1972. 'Fall of East Pakistan: Some economic consequences', *Pakistan Economic and Social Review*, 10(1), 9–16.

Jahan, R. 1972. *Pakistan: Failure in national integration*. New York: Columbia University Press.

Khan, S.R. 2020. *Development economics: A critical introduction*. New York: Routledge.

1 New institutional economics and economic development

Introduction

Explaining the success or failure of nations is an important genre in the literature going back to Adam Smith and before.[1] One narrative that has garnered
much attention pertains to the role of institutions as posited by New Institutional Economics (NIE). This attention is due partly to the academic success
and persuasive writing of the seminal thinkers in the field. Probably for these
reasons, this narrative was adopted by the World Bank, International Monetary Fund (IMF) and other development organizations (Cameron, 2004). It
has subsequently been widely diffused to low- and low-middle-income countries (L/LMICs)[2] via their funding of structural adjustment programs. Since
these two Bretton Woods organizations are among the most influential in the
field of economic development, the narratives that they adopt require close
scrutiny. The seminal contributions to this field, as it pertains to economic
development, are explicated first in this chapter, and that is followed by identifying some gaps in NIE.

Explaining the success or failure of nations[3]

In a nutshell, economists learnt from Smith (1908) that nations progress
due to skill and dexterity of the workforce, enhanced labor force participation rates and because higher labor productivity is induced by the division
of labor and specialization. Capital facilitates the latter via the invention of
machines, which facilitate specialization and constrict the time needed for
manufacturing processes. Accumulation, thus, occurs prior to the division of
labor. Subsequent accumulation enables further specialization, and prosperity
rises proportionately. Capital circulates and transforms itself from money to
goods for production and back into money, and the circuit makes profit for
the employers. For this to occur, nations need tolerable security; otherwise,
there is an incentive to bury capital for contingencies rather than consume it
or employ it for profit (pp. 207–209).

DOI: 10.4324/9781032630878-1

One point from Smith's narrative is particularly noteworthy from the perspective of our research question. He makes a reference to good institutions, and prominent modern explanations of why nations prospered, that is, the prime cause of progress, suggest sound institutions distinguish nations that prospered from those that did not.[4] From a historical economic development perspective of why nations fail or succeed, the writings of Douglass North and Daron Acemoglu and James A. Robinson, respectively, have drawn much attention. Their focus is on the role of institutions in forging social and economic progress, and their contributions are a prominent part of NIE.

Douglass North speculated on why and how some societies grew when they did and why others stagnated.[5] He also developed an analytical framework to explore the process of economic change or the lack of it. The most direct and succinct application of his thinking to economic growth and development is contained in his Gunnar Myrdal Lecture, sponsored by the United Nations Economic Commission for Europe (North, 2003).

In terms of the broader framework that he used, human societies are viewed as distinct from other species in that they are constantly evolving and, as such, manifest no underlying ergodic structure that social science could be directed at revealing (2005, p. 50). The only social constant is that human action changes the physical and human environment (2005, p. 21). Thus, because institutions need to constantly evolve to adapt to the changing environment, there is no guarantee that erstwhile successful institutions would serve well in the future (2005, pp. 124–125). Institutions are defined as formal rules (constitutions, laws and regulations), informal rules (norms and conventions, internally held codes of conduct) and enforcement mechanisms (state, society) (2003, p. 2, 2005, p. 3). Institutions need to be distinguished from organizations defined as economic bodies (firms, trade unions), social bodies (churches, clubs, nonprofit associations) and educational bodies. Organizations and institutions interact to produce the adaptions in the institutional framework for economic success.

North (2015, p. 2) started with micro foundations in which he rejected instrumental rationality. Instead, he posited a society with incomplete and asymmetric information along with limited mental capacity to process information and high enforcement costs. The result is uncertainty and high transaction costs in market exchanges. In this context, mental models are culturally derived via an intergenerational transfer of institutions (norms and values), and clearly, this differs across ethnic groups and societies.[6] Acknowledging Ronald Corse, he argued that institutions evolved in the West to deal with societal constraints to reduce uncertainty in human transactions. Prominent among such institutions are the rule of law, property rights and the enforcement of contracts. Based on these micro foundations, North's key concern was their macro implications, including how they pertained to economic development.

Human society, he argued, is also distinct in manifesting consciousness and "intentionality" in bringing about institutional change to adapt to broader change. Given the various and complex interactions within society, human understanding is limited, and so success in framing new institutions is not guaranteed. Failure might also result from the rigidities militating against institutional change ("rules of the game"), since the organizations ("players") that embody and benefit from the existing institutional structure have a vested interest in preserving it (2005, pp. 53–59).

North did not view neo-classical economics as an appropriate framework to study economic development because it is static, assumes perfect information and zero transactions cost ("a friction-less world") and rejects the idea of intentionality. He concluded that the neo-classical model is better suited to studying resource allocation in high-income economies, that is, where it evolved.

He argued that understanding the world required a complementary understanding of politics, society and cognitive science and also of the evolution of cultural heritage (based on religion, myths, superstitions and prejudices) of particular societies and the associated institutional evolution (2003, p. 1, 2005, p. 18). Institutions facilitate transactions by reducing uncertainty in a world with friction. North acknowledged the importance of preferences, choices, incentives, property rights and markets that are central to neo-classical economics, but their role and importance are theorized differently.[7] Incentives, for example, are considered to be institutions, because they structure human economic interactions and make behavior predictable.

Enforcement is never perfect, since the returns on the margin from enhancing enforcement decline relative to the payoff. However, the degree of imperfection is important, and, in this context, politics frame the rules of the market game (2003, p. 4). Politics also determine to whose advantage the rules are framed. The most fundamental rules concern the ownership, use and alienation of property, as well as the enforcement of contracts (2003, p. 4).

Path dependence can move society toward either prosperity or decline. For example, factors like religion or geography can influence cultural beliefs, which can, in turn, shape good or bad institutions, leading to either good or bad polities (2003, pp. 5–6, 2005, pp. 50, 58). North clarified that path dependence is perpetuated by organizations whose survival depends on the survival of existing institutions, so the concept should not be simplistically interpreted as inertia (2005, p. 51).

Culture represents the intergenerational transfer of norms, values and beliefs. There is a suggestion that religion is endogenous and produces beliefs consistent with the demographic and resource constraints embedded in the geography. For example, the Christian religious framework was suited to the adaptations (institutional and organization changes) congenial to growth. However, the evolution of collectivist rather than the individualist culture that emerged from Muslim religious practice was less suited to impersonal market exchange (2005, pp. 135–136).

The most fundamental transition in human economic interactions is the transition from personal exchange (barter) to impersonal exchange (market).[8] This transition is facilitated by institutions (property rights) and well-functioning organizations that embody these institutions (banks, corporations), as well as enforcement mechanisms (low cost and efficient judicial systems) that boost productivity, induce cooperation and punish defection. States in poor societies fail to achieve this institutional framework and, hence, fail to encourage transactions and economic growth (pp. 134–135). Conversely, in prosperous societies cultural heritage can shape economic and political institutions that facilitate cooperative behavior and hence reduce transactions cost (2003, p. 8, 2005, pp. 18, 135–136).

Order in society reduces uncertainty and hence facilitates transactions. This can be attained at low cost if there is a shared system of norms and beliefs that are consistent with the rule of law and that constrain predatory behavior of individuals and organizations. Western societies benefited from a cultural heritage of participatory and stable political institutions conducive to impersonal exchange with the requisite flexibility to adapt to changes. North traced the historical evolution of these institutions (2005, pp. 107–108). Authoritarianism could work, at least for a while, if the rules imposed by the ruler are viewed by the ruled to be in their self-interest. Many poor societies suffer from the lack of order having neither of these polities (participatory or authoritarian) and are additionally handicapped from having to compete with an already-developed world (2005, p. 120).

North's reflections on policy are terse. In a nutshell, the prosperity of nations depends on formal rules, informal rules and enforcement mechanisms. North argued that only the first of the three is responsive to policy, and hence, policy economists (neo-liberal) who derive their inspiration from neo-classical economics emphasized "getting prices right" and "fell flat on their faces over and over again."[9] For North (2015), such allocative efficiency economics has meaning in the context of an appropriate institutional context that exists in western market economies, but L/LMICs need adaptive efficiency to arrive at the appropriate institutional framework to address the problem of scarcity and the productive competitive pressures that usher.

Like many economic development scholars, North emphasized the importance of learning. He suggested that supporting institutions and complementarities are likely to make a LIC physicist or chemist more productive when based in an HIC, even though the scarcity of these professionals in LICs would lead neo-classical economists to predict the opposite (2003, p. 7). To offset this, he recommended the development of knowledge systems based on the founding of appropriate institutions and organizations – as done in much of East Asia, most recently in China.

North made a very effective critique of neo-liberal structural adjustment programs, arguing that their exclusive focus on formal rules dooms them to fail. Yet he made the observation that LICs need to shift from a society regulated by traditional cultural norms – respect for status and rank, a coercive polity, mutual control and enforced codes of generosity – into an open society with free entry and exit, democratic governance and competence criteria (2005, p. 100). Nonetheless, North (2015, p. 9) conceded that as yet little is known about how adaptive efficiency can be induced in L/LMICs via an appropriate institutional matrix that sets into motion desired dynamic change.

In a co-authored paper (Cox, North and Weingast, 2019) prior to North's passing, ethnic heterogeneity and its potential to undermine development via ethnic conflict are indirectly addressed. The authors argued that natural states prevent violence by providing rents to those with high violence potential. Natural states are defined as polities that distribute rents in order to keep the peace. Rents result from limiting access to outsider individuals or organizations, for example, excluded ethnic groups. This limits their ability to engage in conflict and keeps insiders appeased in a static world. The cost of thus securing peace is the undermining of overall development via various mechanisms, such as the focus on rent creation rather than the most productive activities engaged in via the most productive ways, for example, building a complex interdependent economy via specialization.

However, change, and thus conflict, is inevitable, and so the proposed solution is market-based open access orders (no limits for rent creation) that accompany democratic reforms. This would result in a virtuous cycle of peace, rather than a vicious cycle of conflict (violence trap), that generates the most surplus and creates incentives to avoid conflict as the economy becomes more complex and interdependent. This book welcomes democratic reforms but argues that generating ethnic peace requires more wide-reaching and targeted institution building rather than simply open access market reforms.

Acemoglu and Robinson's (2012) thesis also explored why some countries succeeded and did so employing North's general framework.[10] Acemoglu and Robinson viewed elites as universally prone to predation and self-enrichment. However, development is premised on harnessing the productive potential of much of the nation's population and hence requires inclusive political and economic institutions.[11] Inclusive political institutions evolve historically via different mechanisms and processes in different countries as described by North (see earlier). Also, at critical junctures, small differences can have lasting impacts due to cumulative causation and result in the onset of vicious or virtuous circles. For example, the Black Plague that decimated the population of England and Western Europe strengthened the hand of the peasantry that bid for higher wages.

In England's case, this strengthened the hand of peasants who were providing free labor to oppressive feudal lords. Labor was able to bid for higher wages despite the Monarchy's attempts to restore the old wages and forced labor. By contrast, in Eastern Europe the feudal lords were stronger and more predatory, and even more ferocious feudal oppression emerged to repress the peasantry in what was called "the second serfdom". This difference was enough in leading to a very different historical evolution of institutions and economic growth trajectories in Western and Eastern Europe.

A tradition of resistance was established in England, which was the first to fight for inclusive political institutions and associated economic freedoms. The Civil War of 1642–1651 and the Glorious Revolution of 1688 limited the power of the King and strengthened Parliament. Subsequently, the Monarch had to negotiate to be given tax authority by Parliament and conceded more freedoms in exchange. In addition to reducing the Monarchy's arbitrary authority over matters such as taxation, merchants achieved economic freedoms such as the granting of patents and other property rights and the abolition of monopolies. The establishment of law and order further promoted commerce.

These institutional changes promoting inclusivity set the stage for harnessing scientific breakthroughs for an industrial revolution. Since Parliament won the battle with the Monarch regarding the monopolization of trade, the merchant traders were enriched and used their capital accumulation for industrialization. The unlikely defeat of the Spanish Armada by England is another example of a fortuitous circumstance of great historical significance when the right circumstances and institutions are in place. In this case, it opened up the Atlantic merchant trading to the English and further strengthened the hand of Parliament to hold the Monarchy in check. The French and Spanish equivalents to the British Parliament lost this struggle, and this consolidated England's lead.

The impact of the industrial revolution had differentiated impacts depending on institutional evolution in different parts of the world. There was institutional convergence via different paths and processes in Western Europe and the settler colonies of North America and Oceana, and culturally, these regions were receptive to the diffusion of the industrial revolution. Eastern Europe had adopted an alternative path that had entrenched extractive institutions and was not a receptive ground for such changes until much later. Virtuous circles came into play in Western European countries as inclusive political institutions secured economic freedoms that harnessed the productive potential of most of the populations, and economic growth and prosperity also strengthened political development.

The rest of the world was mired in vicious circles. Predatory institutions enriched only the elites who resisted technological changes that usher in creative destruction and more widespread prosperity and hence threaten their power and privileges. They only adopted military technological changes as instruments of repression. If there was growth, it was based on coercion, but since the latter did not tap the productive potential of the bulk of the population and resisted progressive changes in technology and political development, economic growth was not sustainable. England and other Western European nations did not spread inclusive political and economic institutions to the other regions and nations that they colonized since their interest was only in using these colonies to enrich themselves.

As with North, Acemoglu and Robinson (2019) elaborated further on their thesis by exploring rents. They emphasized again that inclusive political institutions create inclusive economic institutions (open access orders) that, in turn, create "incentives and opportunities for a broad cross section of society". They differed from Cox et al. (2019) in that they viewed rent creation simply as a mechanism for politically empowered elites "to exploit powerless non-elites" and to consolidate the political order for the benefit of insiders. However, more inclusive politics are necessary but not a sufficient condition for more inclusive economic institutions. Elite capture may replace one predatory regime with another as was the case in Zimbabwe. The result of such regime displacement is crony capitalism that distributes rents to consolidate and retain power for insiders and economic stagnation. The alternative resulting from political and hence economic inclusion is an open access economy that relies on widely diffused incentives in a competitive market economy[12] that generates innovation and economic growth.

The prognosis for authoritarian regimes like China is poor in that more inclusive economic institutions are not accompanied by more inclusive political institutions, and so the virtuous cycle of more inclusive economic institutions diffusing economic power and consolidating more inclusive political institutions and vice versa is not on the table. There is more clarity than Cox et al. (2019) in how political change might come about, for example, via collective action (possibly via social movements). However, Acemoglu and Robinson do not even make an oblique reference to ethnic heterogeneity impacting political and economic development as did Cox, North and Weingast.

Addressing gaps in new institutional economics

As earlier indicated, neo-liberal dogma as propagated by development agencies, like the IMF and World Bank and other multilateral development banks, have absorbed NIE policy prescriptions along with their earlier standard prescriptions of market-based reforms. The emphasis is on good governance, which mitigates corruption and includes legal systems that enforce property rights and contracts.[13]

Tamanaha (2015) noted the difficulty in defining institutions and expressed doubts about NIE policy effectiveness, given the context and cultural specificity of informal institutions that interact with formal ones. Schneider and Nega (2016) argued that the neo-classical micro foundations of NIE based on individualistic rational calculation, and therefore the policy prescriptions following from that, are too narrow and inadequately context specific. They pointed out that these prescriptions do not work in sub-Saharan African conditions. For example, they argued that property rights, such as for land, are communal, and culture (via kinship networks) has a bearing both on land ownership and on broader transactions. They pointed to the importance of national unity in ethnically fragmented societies and that institutional development of the kind recommended by NIE might follow from poverty alleviation and broad-based development.

North's policy recommendations seem to amount to saying L/MICs cannot develop without the requisite institutions and that these requisite institutions are a marker of being developed or an HIC. Indeed, his narrative suggests that these institutions are likely to be endogenous to the development process. Furthermore, North's view of gradual change and path dependency suggests that these norms could not be adopted at will, even if they were pre-conditions for development, since they evolve slowly in the appropriate environment that produces the requisite culture.

While these prominent NIE authors have made a very significant contribution to thinking about economic development, there are important gaps when it comes to identifying a prime cause of what might set off the catch-up growth process in L/LMICs. Path dependency plays a role in both narratives. For North, factors like religion and geography determine cultural beliefs, which, in turn, are central to whether good or bad institutions evolve. Religion is viewed as endogenous and produces cultural beliefs consistent with demographic and resource constraints. Good political and economic institutions that evolve over time with the right culture deliver participatory and stable institutions that deliver the rule of law, property rights and contract enforcement and so constrain predatory behavior and facilitate market-based transactions. Getting the appropriate institutions in place is an uphill struggle since vested interests resist change to preserve the status quo they benefit from.

Acemoglu and Robinson's analysis calls for inclusive institutions such that the productive potential of the bulk of the population can be harnessed. This is similar to North's prescription in that, for him, appropriate institutions would require political and economic freedoms for broad-based inclusion. While North emphasized the evolution of the appropriate culture for the birth of good institutions, Acemoglu and Robinson argued that such institutions evolve "based on small differences at critical historical junctures". While good luck plays a part, culture is implicit in this narrative also since they argue that such inclusive institutions were only diffused to western nations that shared a similar culture.

In both cases, there is no obvious policy message for L/LMICs, given the reference to path dependency and the evolution of western culture. Nonetheless, these prominent contributors to NIE did a major service in highlighting what institutions worked. L/LMICs at least do not have to reinvent the wheel since there is now received wisdom on what they need to attain.

However, there is another gap in the NIE narrative. It treats the population of a nation as homogeneous. If that were the case and if L/LMICs could somehow attain similar inclusive institutions that evolved in the West (notwithstanding path dependence and cultural differences), perhaps they can attain catch-up growth. The problem is that, as indicated earlier, many L/LMICs are ethnically fragmented. While the reference to inclusive institutions in the NIE literature is to vertical inclusiveness (across class), in ethnically fragmentated nations, the starting point needs to horizontal (across ethnicity) inclusiveness.[14] In other words, L/LMICs that are ethnically fragmented need to start with building institutions that will deliver both horizontal and vertical equity or inclusion to attain national cohesion, and such cohesion can be a trigger (or prime cause) for catch-up growth.

Political divisiveness based on ethnicity is not easily withstood by many L/MICs, and this gives salience to paying attention to ethnic fragmentation and hence national cohesion as a prime cause. Ethnic identity in more traditional societies, as an ascriptive identity, trumps others. While an outsider may not be able to differentiate one from the other, the members of a group know who is and who is not "one of us". Those of the key ascriptive identity immediately form a connection as strangers in a different geography by speaking the common language.

This provides the plausible explanation for why "natural" nations are more likely to succeed than "constructed" ones, ceteris paribus, since a "natural" social cleavage (structural weakness) has been removed.[15] Political entrepreneurs now have to work much harder to capitalize on cleavages since this natural hook is gone. Once significant ethnic fractionalization is combined with factors like economic inequality, resource maldistribution and perceived or actual ethnic discrimination, it is easier for ethnic entrepreneurs to use ethnicity to perpetrate and reinforce ethnic violence and political instability.

Similarly, the lack of ethnic fragmentation as a social cleavage in a society makes it more likely that policy makers will favor inclusive institutions/policies since the beneficiaries are more likely to be "people like us" rather than "strangers". It is on this premise that the conceptual framework in Chapter 2 shows that most who constitute a natural nation are more likely to act in a unified way as though there is a "collective will" to develop. This lack of easily exploitable social cleavage is even more important in scarcity economies (L/LMICs) where life is more likely to be and perceived to be a zero-sum game than in ethnically fragmented HICs.

The underlying assumption of an inevitable proclivity to predation among leaders in Acemoglu and Johnson is contradicted by many counterexamples within their book and those of other researchers of East Asia development. Examples of nationally motivated enlightened leadership mentioned in the book include Okubo Toshimichi and Shimazu Hisamitsu of Japan, Quett Masire and Seretse Khama of Botswana, the two Roosevelts of the United States, Deng Xiaoping in China and Luiz Inácia Lula of Brazil.[16] Further, fitting East Asia into the same mold as Western Europe for explaining their progress as they do is not persuasive. In fact, the experience of East Asia points to a different explanation for progress and one based on sound leadership, national cohesion and an innovative economic strategy referred to in the development economics literature as developmentalism.

While inclusive political and economic institutions may have emerged as part of the East Asian story, this happened along with and not before catch-up growth occurred. What more likely set off the process of growth was a sense of nationhood, possibly under siege, and the patriotic urge to do better and be ranked among the richer nations. The fact that the East Asian countries referred to (Japan, Korea and Taiwan) were not ethnically fragmented provides more reason for exploring ethnicity and national cohesion.

As argued earlier, colonial history has dealt many L/LMICs a bad hand, and multifarious ethnicities or nations wrapped into one are subject to tensions and strife rather than engaging in creating a sense of nationhood.[17] In such cases, institutional change needs to be consistent with forging national cohesion as explained in Chapter 5. Poor nations with many ethnicities also confront a competition for resources that leads to real and imagined ethnic injustices, undermines the effort to create a sense of nationhood and delays the emergence of collective action for catch-up growth. Centripetal forces forging homogenization and nationhood compete with centrifugal forces of poverty and ethnic strife. In this race against time, good policies that encourage horizontal and vertical inclusion can be an antidote to rifts bred by poverty (Chapter 5).

To sum up, North and Acemoglu and Robinson have put forward very persuasive narratives on why nations succeed or fail. This book argues that, as a complement to their analysis, natural nations that do not have to contend with ethnic strife have an in-built advantage in forging a sense of nationhood. Those not so fortunate have to first engage in the painstaking task of forging a sense of nationhood or national cohesion. How this can be done is suggested in Chapter 5 by drawing on historical examples and case studies.

Summary and conclusion

Seminal thinkers contributing to NIE and economic development focus on institutions that promote economic freedom and facilitate market transactions (e.g., rule of law, property rights, contract enforcement) and political institutions promoting inclusion and broad-based participation. While these institutions are important, they are often endogenous. They are also subject to path dependence, derivative from a particular culture, and therefore evolve in and are diffused in similar cultural contexts.

Notwithstanding the value of these institutions for market-based economies, since L/LMICs have a different history (with colonialism playing a significant role) and a different culture from one that evolved in HICs, they are not *a priori* a fertile ground for recommended NIE institutions. North recognized the inherent policy limitations of the extension of NIE institutions to L/LMICs.

An important colonial legacy for most L/LMICs is the way borders were determined prior to independence and therefore the ethnic fragmentation newly independent nations subsequently had to contend with. NIE deals with institutional evolution in current HICs and hence lacks any real discussion of the importance of ethnicity. The contention in this book that natural nations, where the predominant ethnicity in a defined geographic space virtually includes the whole population, have an advantage in building national cohesion, a prime cause of economic and social progress (Chapter 4).

HICs have had the advantage of time to organically build national cohesion, partly via education and language policy, even if they are not natural nations. Many of these countries are social democracies, and policies that look to the well-being of the less well-off add to the sense of solidarity, inclusion and nationhood. L/LMICs are culturally different, and institution building accordingly needs to differ. Further, institution building in nations that are ethnically fragmented needs to focus initially on horizontal inclusion to build a sense of nationhood (Chapter 5).

Finally, there is a need to situate the contribution of this book within the broader literature on why nations succeed or fail. Acemoglu and Robinson and North, explicitly or implicitly, concede that contextual factors limit the policy relevance of their analysis. As Macleod (2013, p. 4) pointed out, this puts the analysis "in the realm of omitted variable bias". The thesis proposed in this book is an attempt to address this omitted variable bias by addressing ethnic heterogeneity and its association with national cohesion and hence with social and economic progress. This has a bearing on the nature of institution building that needs to take precedence.

Notes

1 For example, Ibn Khaldun (2005), a fourteenth-century Tunisian sociologist of Arab descent, presented a theory of history that dealt with a prime cause for development.
2 The broad concern of this book is with catch-up growth. Since middle-income countries (MICs) have attained some measure of catch-up growth to attain middle-income status, although sustaining it is a challenge, given the concerns about a middle-income trap (Khan, 2020, Chapter 10), my focus is on L/LMICs.
3 This section draws on Khan (2014).
4 For similarities in North's conceptual framework with that of Smith's, including the critical role of institutions, refer to Kim (2014).
5 For a chronological review of North's many contributions (from the 1960s to 2015), refer to Hodgson (2017). For a more specific contribution of North to NIE, refer to Menard and Shirley (2014). For a discussion of the relation of North's contribution to "old institutional economics" (OIE), refer to Dugger (1995). For a Marxist critique of North's theoretical framework, some of which Hodgson (2017) took issue with, refer to Milonakis and Fine (2005). Vandenberg (2002) distinguished NIE from neoclassical economics, and Gagliardi (2008) discussed the different strands and substrands in the NIE literature as did Leite et al. (2014) from an economic development perspective. Refer to Castellano and García-Quero (2012) for the debates ushered into development economics by NIE scholars. Gorodnichenko and Roland (2017) complemented North's analysis by empirically showing that culture, specifically individualism and the status accorded to individual achievement, boosts discovery and innovation and accounts for the higher growth and wealth of western nations.
6 For more on mental models, refer to Shughart et al. (2020).
7 North argued that cognitive science assumes importance for choice made under conditions of imperfect information. Also refer to (1990, chapter 3) for a discussion of behavioral assumptions and individual behavior.

8 North referred to overlapping innovations that reduce transactions cost by raising capital mobility, reducing information costs and diffusing risk (1990, pp. 125–130).
9 North is likely to have been influential in the formulation of the second generation of structural adjustment reforms instituted by the Breton Woods organizations emphasizing "good governance".
10 Grinberg (2018) contests Acemoglu and Robinson's theoretical framework and also their empirical findings in a couple of case studies to dispute the thesis about the formation and effectiveness of inclusive institutions. The authors used a Marxist framework of global capital accumulation to view national developmental and institutional patterns. Dzionek-Kozlowska and Matera (2021) contest the lack of the role of culture (informal institutions) in Acemoglu and Robinson's earlier writings and review the changing role culture plays in their later work.
11 Menocal (2017, p. 561) defined inclusive institutions "in terms of both process (e.g., how decisions are made) and outcomes (e.g., development that is more broadly shared)". The issue of how states and societies could transform themselves in ways that are more inclusive, open and representative was also addressed in the paper.
12 Acemoglu and Robinson conceded the importance of market failures including attempts at securing monopoly rents. They pointed out that high-income western countries have for now political institutions that are strong enough to thwart such attempts, while this is not the case in L/LMICs. For example, they pointed out that in essence, Bill Gates of Microsoft had identical predatory instincts as did Carlos Slim of Mexico. However, while the US federal regulators sued Microsoft and blocked its monopolization attempts, Carlos Slim's monopolization of telecommunications actually had legislative cover.
13 Refer to Jean-Marie Badlands et al. (2020) for contributions to several aspects of the burgeoning institutions and development sub-field by prominent development economists. NIE has also ushered in a spate of empirical research that explores how institutional quality, defined variously as quality of governance (democracy, judiciary, transparency etc.), rule of law and protection of property rights and hence constraints on predatory politics, is positively associated with economic growth (via various mechanisms such as foreign investment, foreign aid, financial development, innovation, entrepreneurship and remittances), poverty reduction and the environmental improvement.
14 Stewart (2000) emphasized this point as indicated in Chapter 3.
15 Political entrepreneurs can also exploit and reinforce other social cleaves based on religion, sect, class and ideology. Thus, depending on the source of the problem, institution building needs to be flexible and to address crises as they arise. However, as indicated by Chapter 3, ethnic fragmentation is a problem many L/LMICs need to address first. I would like to thank an anonymous reviewer for the points in the highlighted paragraphs.
16 North also alludes to the importance of good leadership.
17 Some ethnic groups like the Kurds, Palestinians and Kashmiris have a highly developed sense of nationhood but not the land or political freedom to exercise catch-up growth. Myrdal (1956, p. 3) was concerned about integration and hoped development would facilitate national integration in underdeveloped countries and how this might facilitate international integration. Almost seven decades later, this remains a critical issue in L/LMICs.

References

Acemoglu, D. and Robinson, J.A. 2012. *The origins of power, prosperity, and poverty: Why nations fail*. New York: Crown Business.
Acemoglu, D. and Robinson, J.A. 2019. 'Rents and economic development: The perspective of why nations fail', *Public Choice*, 181(1), 13–28.

Cameron, J.D. 2004. 'The World Bank and the New institutional economics: Contradictions and implications for development policy in Latin America', *Latin American Perspectives*, 31(4), 97–103.

Castellano, F.L. and García-Quero, F. 2012. 'Institutional approaches to economic development: The current status of the debate', *Journal of Economic Issues*, 46(4), 921–940.

Cox, G.W., North, D.C. and Weingast, B.R. 2019. 'The violence trap: A political-economic approach to the problems of development', *Journal of Public Finance and Public Choice*, 34(1), 3–19.

Dugger, W.M. 1995. 'Douglass C. North's new institutionalism', *Journal of Economic Issues*, 29(2), 453–458.

Dzionek-Kozlowska, J. and Matera, R. 2021. 'Institutions without culture: On Daron Acemoglu and James Robinson's theory of economic development', *Journal of Economic Issues*, 55(3), 656–676.

Gagliardi, F. 2008. 'Institutions and economic change: A critical survey of the new institutional approaches and empirical evidence', *The Journal of Socio-Economics*, 37(1), 416–443.

Gorodnichenko, Y. and Roland, G. 2017. 'Culture, institutions, and the wealth of nations', *The Review of Economics and Statistics*, 99(3), 402–416.

Grinberg, N. 2018. 'Institutions and capitalist development: A critique of the new institutional economics', *Science & Society*, 82(2), 203–233.

Hodgson, G.M. 2017. 'Introduction to the Douglass C. North memorial issue', *Journal of Institutional Economics*, 13(1), 1–23.

Khaldun, I. 2005. *Muqaddimah: An introduction to history*. Princeton, NJ: Bollingen Series, Princeton University Press.

Khan, S.R. 2014. *A history of development economics thought: Challenges and counter-challenges*. New York: Routledge.

Khan, S.R. 2020. *Development economics: A critical introduction*. New York: Routledge.

Kim, K. 2014. 'Adam Smith's and Douglass North's multidisciplinary approach to economic development', *The American Journal of Economics and Sociology*, 73(1), 3–31.

Leite, D.N., Silva, S.T. and Afonso, O. 2014. 'Institutions, economics and the development quest', *Journal of Economic Surveys*, 28(3), 491–515.

MacLeod, W.B. 2013. 'On economics: A review of why nations fail by D. Acemoglu and J. Robinson and pillars of prosperity by T. Besley and T. Persson', *Journal of Economic Literature*, 51(1), 116–143.

Menard, C. and Shirley, M.M. 2014. 'The contribution of Douglass North to new institutional economics', in Galiani, S. and Sened, I. (eds.) *Institutions, property rights, and economic growth: The legacy of Douglass North*. New York: Cambridge University Press.

Menocal, A.R. 2017. 'Political settlements and the politics of transformation: Where do 'inclusive institutions' come from? *Journal of International Development*, 29(5), 559–575.

Milonakis, D. and Fine, B. 2005. 'Douglass North's remaking of economic history: A critical appraisal', *Review of Radical Political Economics*, 39(1), 27–57.

Myrdal, G. 1956. *An international economy*. New York: Harper & Brothers Publishers.

North, D.C. 1990. *Institutions, institutional change and performance*. Cambridge: Cambridge University Press.

North, D.C. 2003. *The role of institutions in economic development. Gunnar Myrdal Lecture. Occasional Paper No. 1.* New York and Geneva: Economic Commission for Europe, United Nations.

North, D.C. 2005. *Understanding the process of economic change.* Princeton, NJ: Princeton University Press.

North, D.C. 2015. 'The new institutional economics and development', in Krug, B. (ed.), *State capitalism.* Northampton, MA: Elgar, 335–342.

Schneider, G. and Nega, B. 2016. 'Limits of the new institutional economics approach to African development', *Journal of Economic Issues*, 50(2), 435–443.

Shughart, W.F. II, Thomas, D.W. and Thomas, M.D. 2020. 'Institutional change and the importance of understanding shared mental models', *Kyklos*, 73(3), 371–391.

Smith, A. 1908. *An inquiry into the nature and causes of the wealth of nations.* London: George Routledge & Sons.

Stewart, F. 2000. 'Crisis prevention: Tackling horizontal inequalities', *Oxford Development Studies*, 28(3), 245–262.

Tamanaha, B.Z. 2015. 'The knowledge and policy limits of new institutional economics on development', *Journal of Economic Issues*, 49(1), 89–109.

Vandenberg, P. 2002. 'North's institutionalism and the prospect of combining theoretical approaches', *Cambridge Journal of Economics*, 26(2), 217–235.

2 Nations, conceptual framework and method

Introduction

Since the distinction between natural (90 percent or more common ethnicity) and constructed nations is a central feature of this book, this chapter starts with clarifying the difference. This distinction also plays into the main research question explored in this book i.e., what if any role does this distinction between natural and constructed nations play in explaining the success of nations. The conceptual framework for this research question follows and finally the methods for gathering and providing evidence pertaining to this research question is presented.

Natural and constructed nations

A natural nation is defined as a population that coheres based on a common ethnicity.[1] If such a nation shares a common religion and sect, then the cohesion can be even greater, and this condition is referred to as national cohesion. Nations that do not conform to the definition above are viewed as constructed nations. Constructed nations are often a product of colonialism and generally represent an amalgam of ethnicities. Post-colonial borders, crafted by colonial powers, paid no heed to the determinants of national cohesion when constructing nations.

The proposition this book is concerned with is that natural nations, based on shared ethnicity,[2] usually associated with shared language, biology, heritage, history (common origin), culture, habits, norms, values, race and possibly religion, are less likely to be mired in conflict, compared to nations constructed by colonial rule, which are an amalgam of ethnicities.[3] Since ethnicity often, though not always,[4] encompasses the other commonalities, ethnicity is used as the key identity marker to represent all the others.[5] The national cohesion resulting from a shared ethnicity is likely to produce more widely targeted social investments, prosperity and equality, that is, development.

The impact of ethnicity on economic growth and other development indicators has been well researched, as will become evident in the literature review

DOI: 10.4324/9781032630878-2

in Chapter 3.[6] However, there is an innate policy limitation to the expected findings of this research, important as it is to try to discover what impedes the progress of nations. If, in this regard, ethnic fragmentation is problematic as several scholars have pointed out, there is little that can be done peacefully to ethnically defragment nations. However, it is possible to create national cohesion despite the fragmentation in constructed nations, and that is what this book works toward.

National cohesion may be a trigger for catch-up growth as noted in the Preface. Social and economic inclusions are posited to result from a sense of fraternity and common destiny shared by a common ethnicity such that elites view investing in *all* citizens as natural and necessary for the common endeavor of attaining catch-up growth.

Nations that more recently (using a historical frame) experienced catch-up growth, such as Japan, South Korea and Taiwan, engaged in building politically, economically and socially inclusive institutions, simultaneously, with increasing prosperity. Recovering from defeat (Japan) or attaining security via economic strength (South Korea and Taiwan) can be viewed as nationally shared goals by patriotic[7] citizens. These countries represent some examples of shared ethnicities that attained and sustained catch-up growth and shared prosperity. Ethnically homogeneous Bangladesh was discounted by political observers as a basket case, but a spirit of common endeavor and patriotism could have done much to prove the world wrong as it embarked on catch-up growth.

Natural nations do not always have a territory they can claim to realize their potential. Kashmiris, Kurds and the Palestinians are examples of ethnicities denied a territory. North America, before the arrival of Caucasians (whites), was inhabited by natural nations with their unique language, customs and laws. While they marked their territories, they did not have borders in the sense of modern nation-states. However, the reference to First Nations by the Canadian government is in this regard accurate, while a reference to these natural nations as tribes in the United States diminishes what they represented or represent. Several natural African nations were nomadic, and some like the Maasai and Samburu continue to resist state attempts to make them sedentary.

Sometimes ethnicities can successfully struggle to become natural nations as was the case of Bangladesh discussed in the Preface. However, it is more common that such struggles by ethnicities to become natural nations are thwarted by the dominant ethnicity as was the case in the liberation struggle (1967–1970) by the Igbo ethnic group in Nigeria to create Biafra or the liberation struggle (1976–2009) of the Tamils in Sri Lanka to establish Eelam. Such struggles continue even in prosperous nations, though in more mature democracies, such struggles could be peaceful as is the case with Scotland and Catalina in Spain. This, however, was not the case with the Basque liberation struggle in Spain (1959–2011).

While this book is not concerned with high-income countries (HICs), they may have much to teach low- and low-middle-income countries (L/LMICs) about national cohesion. A good example of how national cohesion can be constructed is the famous melting pot of the United States. While, usually over a generation, immigrants adopt the broader common culture, this does not preclude a continued attachment to the ethnic culture of origin. Hence, the wide use of hyphenations such as Chinese-American, Indian-American and Italian-American and so on.

A war of liberation and struggles against nature and natives forged a unity among Caucasians and a sense of nationhood in the United States. Over time, the country opened itself to diverse ethnicities for human power and via culture, education and sports, among other social features, built and sustained a sense of greater inclusion and nationhood over time. While such inclusion has been slow in coming, and certainly much more is needed, for example, for native inhabitants of the land and blacks and other non-Caucasians, some progress has been made. Nation building in the United States could be referred to as organic construction. Post-colonial national construction in L/LMICs for the most part did not have the same leisure of time and resources, and the attempts to forge national cohesion in this regard are generally inorganic but necessary (Chapter 5).

As western democratic nations have prospered, inclusion via social democracy has been enhanced, and ethnicity has become less of an issue and political divisions based on ideology more so. Even so, ethnic tensions do not entirely disappear, as evident from the example of Spain, the (now) more muted tensions between the Dutch- and French-speaking communities in Belgium or the resentments of Quebec nationalists in Canada.

The United States, again, presents an example of how divisiveness based on ethnicity can come into play even if a melting pot militates toward a common culture. The US Census predicted that Caucasians will become a minority in the United States by 2045.[8] Predictions like this opened the door for political entrepreneurs and populists like Donald Trump to campaign on an anti-immigration platform targeted at predominantly a Caucasian base.[9] Notwithstanding the political divisiveness created by political opportunists in the United States, institutions seem strengthened enough to withstand threats to democracy from Trumpian politics. Unfortunately, political divisiveness based on ethnicity is not as easily withstood by many L/LMICs.

As Hettne (1993) pointed out, the state may be associated with or captured by the dominant ethnic group, and challenges to this group may be viewed as anti-state. The antipathy in the Bangladeshi war of liberation was predominantly against the Punjabi ethnic group that dominated the military, civil and other services. Similarly, the Balochi nationalism currently targets the Punjabi ethnic group that is viewed as predatory and as having captured the state (see Chapters 4 and 5).

To sum up, this book argues that natural nations that do not have to contend with ethnic strife have an in-built advantage in forging a sense of nationhood. Those not so fortunate have to first engage in the painstaking task of forging a sense of nationhood or national cohesion. This book suggests how this can be done by drawing on historical examples and case studies in Chapter 5. I turn in the next section to presenting a conceptual framework to examine the thesis proffered here.

Conceptual framework

Economists for the most part believe that individuals act in their self-interest as rational beings. Using jargon, all individuals have a utility (benefit) function, and their behavior shows they act to maximize their own well-being subject to the income they possess as a constraining factor. Moving from the individual to household behavior is more complicated since individuals within the household may have different utility functions. Economists often make the simplifying assumption that the head of the household acts to maximize household well-being, but this is controversial if utility functions within the household are not identical. Moving from the household to the national level, in considering decision making, obviously enhances the complexity multifold, if not infinitely, even for natural nations.

To proceed then, it would be necessary to assume that most who constitute a natural nation act in a unified way as though there is a collective will and that this is not the case for constructed nations. While this would be difficult, if not impossible, to establish conclusively, examples that suggest that collective will, or the lack of it, may be at play are first presented, and then how one could go about testing for its possible presence methodologically is indicated. The example pertains to how Bangladesh managed to contain its population growth once it gained independence compared to Pakistan's inability to achieve a similar result.[10] Table 2.1 shows Bangladesh's and Pakistan's population in selected years.

Table 2.1 shows that at the time of independence in 1971, Bangladesh's (East Pakistan's) population at 65 million was greater than that of West Pakistan at 60 million. Yet, at the terminal year (2021) for which data are available, Bangladesh's population at 165 million was 60 million less than that of Pakistan. As one would expect, following from Table 2.1, a much more rapid decline in fertility rate occurred in Bangladesh relative to Pakistan. Bangladesh's fertility rate (births per woman) declined to 1.99 (below the

Table 2.1 Bangladesh's and Pakistan's population and fertility rates

	Population (millions)		Fertility rates (births per woman)	
Country	1971	2021	1971	2020
Bangladesh	65.53	164.69	6.94	1.99
Pakistan	59.73	225.20	6.60	3.39

Source: Data from database: World Development Indicators, update June 30, 2022.

replacement rate of 2.1), while Pakistan's rate of 3.4 points to a continued and unsustainable population expansion.

The demographic literature discussed in Khan (2022, Chapter 7) explores both demand and supply side explanations for the fertility decline in Bangladesh. Easy explanations, such as religion and policy shortcomings, can be ruled out. Both countries are predominantly Muslim, and it was, in fact, a West Pakistani military dictator, General Ayub Khan, who introduced population planning in both East Pakistan and West Pakistan.

A possible explanation for why there was a much greater acceptance of birth control falls in the realm of speculation that pertains to the main theme of this book, that is, the distinction between natural and constructed nations. When Bangladesh was part of Pakistan, as East Pakistan, there was a collective incentive to enhance its population growth since resource allocation and political power depended on that. Once it gained independence, this incentive dissipated for a nation with the highest population density in the world, that is, their collective incentive was for fertility reduction. Policy makers did their part on the supply side, and the natural nation with a common ethnicity responded.

By contrast, West Pakistan, now Pakistan, remained a constructed nation in which each major province had a different dominant ethnicity. There was little incentive to contain population growth as in Bangladesh. For example, Punjab, the province of the dominant ethnicity of Punjabis, maintains that resources awarded by the National Finance Commission should be based on population. The other provinces have a different take on this. Balochistan has the smallest population but the largest land area and maintains that allocation should be based on land area (Jaffery and Sadaqat, 2006; also see Chapter 5).

Suggesting that national cohesion of natural nations promotes economic development implies that there exists a collective will, as earlier stated.[11] Further, there exists a social welfare function that represents their collective consciousness and will.[12] Based on these propositions, it is possible to summarize these findings. Prior to independence, population entered the social welfare function with a positive sign. Thus, for the East Pakistani Bengali ethnicity, a higher population resulted in higher net well-being collectively since political power (via votes) and resource distribution depended on that. Once East Pakistan became independent, these collective positives disappeared, and the negative impact of population growth on individual and collective well-being became dominant in the changing social milieu, and a rapid fertility decline followed based on individual and collective (policy) decisions.

Testing if this national will in the form of national cohesion in natural nations promotes a common endeavor of attaining national objectives is difficult to engage in empirically because of definitional issues and measurement problems. For example, how is national cohesion to be defined and measured? Can social scientists rely on subjective responses regarding individual motivations? Even so, we know that a national spirit may exist even in constructed nations, though perhaps not to the same extent, based on how fervently fans root for national teams.[13] Nonetheless, due to definitional and measurement problems, the impact of national cohesion in attaining catch-up growth needs to be tested based on outcomes.

This is like Friedman's (1953) methodological assertion that economic agents do not consciously maximize (utility as consumers or profits as producers), but it is possible to test that they do based on outcomes. Thus, if natural nations, based on a common ethnicity, consistently perform better on social and economic outcomes than a control group of constructed nations, this could represent suggestive evidence on the importance of national cohesion in forging economic development. Chapter 4 explores this suggestive evidence based on case studies. The evidence based on cross-country multivariate analysis is reported in Chapter 3, though this too is suggestive given the shortcomings of cross-country multivariate analysis (see Chapter 3, endnote 15).

Methodology

Various methods are used to present evidence pertaining to the research question, that is, the impact of national cohesion on economic development. Chapter 3 relies on a literature review to identify the positive association of ethnic diversity and conflict. This is supported with a tabular review using recent data. A literature review is also used to identify the negative impact of ethnic diversity on economic and social development.

Chapter 4 relies on the descriptive method to contrast socio-economic development in Bangladesh and Pakistan. This comparison comes close to a natural experiment, in that Bangladesh (East Pakistan) and West Pakistan were part of the same country, that is, Pakistan.

We show how East Pakistan was a lagging region and far behind West Pakistan in all social and economic indicators. However, after independence in 1971, in half a century, Bangladesh dominated Pakistan in all social and economic indicators. We attribute the difference to the relative national cohesion in Bangladesh that followed from their being a natural nation where one ethnic group (Bengalis) is predominant (98 percent of the population). By contrast, Pakistan continues to face the strife that comes from the struggle of at least six notable ethnicities. We provide descriptive data analysis that rules out the New Institutional Economics narrative because the prescribed institutional development in Bangladesh lags behind that of Pakistan on all indicators.

Of course, the sense of nationhood that independence brings about can provide a boost to social and economic indicators. We test if that is the case using descriptive statistics and time series analysis to follow the progress of Balkan nations after they declared independence in the early 1990s and 2000s.

The case of Bangladesh is an anomaly. In most cases, natural nations seek-ing self-determination, including their own territory, are stymied by dominant ethnicities or states unwilling to accept an erosion of their territory and associ-ated resources. Also, most L/LMIC nations are colonial constructs and have to contend with the history which includes inter-ethnic strife. In Chapter 5, case studies are used to indicate how constructed nations can forge a sense of nationhood or national cohesion and how this helps with their socio-economic development.

Summary and conclusion

The contention in this book that natural nations, where the predominant eth-nicity in a defined geographic space virtually includes the whole population, have an advantage in building national cohesion, a prime cause of economic and social progress. HICs have had the advantage of time to organically build national cohesion, partly via education and language policy, even if they are not natural nations. Many of these countries are social democracies, and policies that look to the well-being of the less well-off add to the sense of solidarity, inclusion and nationhood. L/LMICs are culturally different, and institution building accordingly needs to differ. Further, institution building in nations that are ethnically fragmented needs to focus initially on horizontal inclusion to build a sense of nationhood (Chapter 5).

Political and social revolutions can change the economic trajectory of nations if inclusive political and economic institutions emerge from them. The Arab Spring indicates the immense resistance that existing political, administrative and military elites mount to protect their privileges. In Egypt's case, subterfuge was used to diffuse the social mobilization, and then via rearguard action, the military reasserted the old order. It seems that dictators become symbols of repressive regimes, and removing them becomes confused with the more difficult goal of changing the predatory system. A social revolution in this regard is a terrible thing to waste, given the enormous cost in terms of the loss of life and well-being and so the need for a focus and insistence on attaining the right objective.

Also, inclusive institutions can be rolled back after decades or even centuries. For example, in the United States, elite education and political power are increas-ingly being monopolized by the very wealthy. The financial and later techno-logical concentration at the turn of the twenty-first century echoed the industrial concentration of the robber baron period of the late nineteenth century. These trends have created income inequality and marginalized talent, and this can fos-ter political instability and undermine economic growth. The political system in the United States is still robust and saw pushback in the form of the "occupy" movement. Political mobilizations and social movements can reverse destructive trends when they use available democratic institutions that the 'occupy move-ment' seemed to have shunned and the 'tea party movement' embraced.

A conceptual framework, illustrated by fertility decline in Bangladesh, is presented to suggest how collective will might come into play in natural nations for social and economic progress. The collection and presentation of evidence as identified in the methodology section is framed by this conceptualization. The main message of this book is that nation-building institutions should come first as a prime cause of development, and they are likely to be initially more important than the institution building policies proposed by New Institutional Economics, which are in any case likely to be endogenous to or accompany social and economic development.

Notes

1 A natural nation was defined in the Preface arbitrarily as one where the dominant ethnicity constitutes 90 percent or more of the population. Harris (1992) pointed out that the term "ethnicity" is derived from the Greek *ethnos* or nation.

2 Ethnicity is used instead of tribe or clan because it is broader, and several tribes and clans can share a common ethnicity. For example, the Pushtun or Baloch ethnicities in Pakistan include several tribes. Ethnicity may, but in most cases does not, overlap with class. For a discussion of different views of ethnicity and conceptual and measurement problems associated with it, refer to Brown (2010).

3 Michalopoulos and Papaioannou (2016) estimate the ongoing negative impact, in terms of generating violence, resulting from borders forged by colonial powers with apparently little thought to the likely future impact of splitting ethnicities.

4 Religion and even sect can vary within an ethnicity, and this may lead to less harmony. For example, Bengalis in East (Muslims) and West Bengal (Hindus) share the same ethnicity but differ in religion.

5 Madan (1998) treats ethnicity from an anthropological perspective as not only an identity marker but also a set of varying strategies to attain statehood. In the latter conceptualization, ethnicity is mutable, at least in the medium term. Canelasa and Gisselquiste (2018) also view ethnicity as mutable and argue for treating it as a dependent rather than an independent variable. Refer to Adlparvar and Tadros (2016) for the four main theoretical approaches (primordialism, instrumentalism, materialism and constructionism) that underpin the study of ethnicity in the social sciences.

6 In *The White Man's Burden* (2006), written for the general reader, Easterly even uses the term "natural" nations in quotes and, in later scholarship, refers to "artificial" nations, though I prefer the term "constructed" nations. In fact, in Chapter 8 of the cited book here, Easterly narrated how nations were constructed by colonialists to serve their own interests with little thought to the future difficulties; in terms of ethnic strife, they were condemning these nations too. In another reading, Easterly cited Pakenham (1991) for details on this process.

7 The distinction commonly made between patriotism and nationalism is relevant here. Patriotism is benign and has an internal focus of enhancing national well-being. Nationalism, by contrast, could have an external focus, and xenophobia is often associated with it.

8 www.brookings.edu/book/diversity-explosion-2/, consulted March 30, 2022.

9 www.vox.com/2020/11/7/21551364/white-trump-voters-2020, consulted March 30, 22.

10 The following paragraphs on fertility decline in Bangladesh are based on Khan (2022, Chapter 7).

11 Populist leaders can, of course, forge and manipulate a collective will via charisma and propaganda. There is a difference since the reference here is to spontaneous rather than induced action.

12 This is where Arrow's (1950) impossibility theorem comes into play.

13 Refer to Chapter 5 for an example of how national support for national teams in constructed nations can be limited due to ethnic conflict.

References

Adlparvar, N. and Tadros, M. 2016. 'The evolution of ethnicity theory: Intersectionality, geopolitics and development', *Institute of Development Studies Bulletin*, 47(2), 123–136.

Arrow, K.J. 1950. 'A difficulty in the concept of social welfare', *Journal of Political Economy*, 58(4), 328–346.

Brown, G.K. and Langer, A. 2010. 'Conceptualizing and measuring ethnicity', *Oxford Development Studies*, 38(4), 411–436.

Canelasa, C. and Gisselquistc, R.M. 2018. 'Horizontal inequality as an outcome', *Oxford Development Studies*, 46(3), 305–324.

Easterly, W. 2006. *The White man's burden: Why the west's efforts to aid the rest have done so much ill and so little good.* New York: Penguin Books.

Friedman, M. 1953. *Essays in positive economics.* Chicago, IL: University of Chicago Press.

Harris, W.A. 1992. 'Ethnicity and development: A review essay', *Social and Economic Studies*, 41(4), 225–230.

Hettne, B. 1993. 'Ethnicity and development – an elusive relationship', *Contemporary South Asia*, 2(2), 123–150.

Jaffery, N.G. and Sadaqat, M. 2006. 'NFC AWARDS commentary and agenda', *Pakistan Economic and Social Review*, 44(2), 209–234.

Khan, S.R. 2022. *South Asian success stories: A story of partnerships.* New York: Routledge.

Madan, T.N. 1998. 'Coping with ethnicity in South Asia: Bangladesh, Punjab and Kashmir compared', *Ethnic and Racial Studies*, 21(5), 969–989.

Michalopoulos, S. and Papaioannou, E. 2016. 'The long-run effects of the scramble for Africa', *American Economic Review*, 106(7), 1802–1848.

Pakenham, T. 1991. *The scramble for Africa.* New York: Random House.

3 Ethnicity and development

Introduction

This chapter first explores the incidence of ethnicity and ethnic conflict in low- and middle-income countries (L/MICs)[1] following from the hypothesis that ethnic diversity[2] in constructed nations results in conflict and undermines national cohesion. The literature on ethnicity and economic development is reviewed next to explore if and the extent to which diverse ethnicities in constructed nations undermine economic growth and development.

Ethnicity, conflict and impacts[3]

Bates (1999) argued that while ethnicity can be a positive force for development (see later), competition between ethnic groups can turn violent (demonstrations, riots, assassinations, revolts, coups[4]). He made use of a dataset containing economic, social and political information on 46 African countries over the period of 1970–1995. He argued that ethnic politics was most volatile when an ethnic bloc was sufficient in size to permanently exclude others from the exercise of power.

Østby's (2008) analysis is based on a dataset constructed from the Demographic and Health Surveys (DHS) for 39 developing countries in the period of 1986–2004. Aggregated macro indicators of polarization and horizontal inequalities were constructed, and the main findings are that social polarization and horizontal social inequality are positively associated with the outbreak of conflict.

Based on new geo-coded data on administrative units in 31 federal states between 1991 and 2005, Deiwiks et al. (2012) demonstrated that regional inequality affected the risk of secessionist conflict particularly when regions had a distinct ethnic identity. In addition, they provided evidence that exclusion from central state power and ethnic groups' access to regional institutions were associated with an increased risk of secession. They showed that both relatively affluent (complaints regarding over-subsidization of low-income

DOI: 10.4324/9781032630878-3

regions) and underdeveloped regions (complaints of exploitation) in federations had an increased risk of secessionist conflict compared to regions that are closer to the country's average wealth.

Esteban et al.'s (2012) empirical study included 138 countries over the period of 1960–2008. They found that ethnic polarization had a large and highly significant impact on conflict across a number of different specifications. This was also true of ethnic fractionalization, in the empirics, though not to the same level of consistency.[5]

Bosker and de Ree (2014) found that only ethnic wars tend to spill over across international borders and that they are more likely to spread along ethnic lines. In the presence of ethnic links, a neighbor at ethnic civil war increased the probability of an outbreak of ethnic civil war on the home territory by four to six percentage points. Not surprisingly, resources can also play a role in ethnic conflict. Wegenast and Basedau (2014) showed that an ethnic fractionalization index, based on the politically relevant groups, was associated with an increased risk of ethnic violence onset, particularly so in oil-rich settings.

Bang and Mitra (2013) showed that the out-migration of highly skilled labor (brain drain) to the Organization for Economic Cooperation and Development (OECD) countries for the period of 1975–2000 was associated with ethnic conflict, much more so than non-ethnic conflict.

Langer et al. (2017) constructed a composite social cohesion index (SCI) based on responses on various rounds of the Afro barometer surveys (2005, 2008 and 2012). The three components of the index were based on elicited perceptions on inequality, trust and identity. The SCI was also adjusted based on the variation in the SCI across ethnic groups. Using data for a variety of conflict events, the authors found a significant relationship between both measures and violent conflict in the subsequent year.

Appendix Tables 3.1(a–c) show how ethnic fragmentation is associated with ethnic conflict in L/MICs.[6] To sum up the findings in Appendix Tables 3.1(a–c), it is clear that many constructed nations continue to have a major challenge on their hands with regard to the coping with varied ethnicities while creating national cohesion. Using 90 percent of total population belonging to the dominant ethnicity as a cut-off for defining a natural nation, 11, 28 and 26 percent, respectively, of low-, low-middle- and upper-middle-income countries (LIC, LMIC, UMIC) could be considered natural.[7] The remaining are constructed, and of these 88, 90 and 49 percent are confronting or have confronted ethnic conflict or civil war in low-, low-middle- and upper-middle-income countries, respectively. Natural nations, as defined earlier, have also confronted ethnic unrest or civil war. This is the case for two of the three low-income natural nations (Sudan and the Yemen Republic) but less so in the case of LMICs and UMICs – 53 and 20 percent, respectively.

Some other facts are evident from Appendix Tables 3.1(a–c). Of the 28 countries classified as low-income by the World Bank, 24 are African, and 22 of these have or are experiencing ethnic conflict. This also highlights the two, Malawi and Zambia, that have avoided ethnic conflict, and detailed case studies of them could be instructive. Although causality cannot be inferred from these tabulations, ethnic conflict in general seems to recede as income or development levels increase. The next section reviews the literature to identify the impact of ethnic fragmentation on social and economic development.

Ethnicity and economic development: literature review[8]

In keeping with the focus of this book, studies on the macro association of ethnicity and development have been reviewed. There is also a vast literature on ethnicity and development, not reviewed, such as those that provide valuable insights on the myriad mechanisms for this association on a micro level. Also not reviewed is the literature treating inter-ethnic (horizontal) inequality as the dependent variable (e.g., Canelasa and Gisselquist, 2018).

While much of the literature reviewed identifies the negative impact of ethnic diversity on development (ethnic debt), particularly in an African context,[9] some report evidence of diversity having a positive impact (ethnic dividend). Bates (1999) argued that ethnic groups could advance the private fortunes of their members by promoting education, urban migration and rural development. Further, ethnicity provided the means for rendering inter-generational contracts binding and thereby promoted private investment. They also provided the means for mobilizing private resources for public purposes and hence promoted the formation of public goods.

Repkine (2014) found a positive association between ethnic diversity and productive efficiency and political stability and speculated on possible causes. He also cited several other studies indicating a positive social, economic and political role of ethnic diversity. Montalvo and Reynal-Querol (2020) noted that earlier findings showed a positive association in smaller units like cities where diversity enhances productivity and replicated these findings. Thus, as unit size increased, the costs of heterogeneity such as lower trust and higher transaction costs kicked in. Applying their empirical model to Africa, they showed diversity could produce higher trade between ethnicities, due to specialization by ethnicity, across constructed borders.

However, the vast bulk of studies on ethnicity and development have shown a negative impact.[10] Several scholars have utilized cross-country regression analysis to arrive at tentative conclusions concerning the association of ethnic fragmentation and per capita GDP growth and other development-related variables of interest. Building on earlier research conducted by Easterly and Levine (1997), Alesina et al. (2003) used updated and disaggregated measures of ethnolinguistic fragmentation[11] (ethnic, linguistic and religious) and suggested a likely negative impact of such fragmentation on per capita GDP growth.

Rodrik (1999) explored the effect of external shocks on growth and showed that the negative impact is larger when the latent social conflicts are greater, including ethnic fragmentation, in an economy and its institutions of conflict management are weaker. The evidence, based on cross-country regression analysis for 1960–1975 and 1975–1989, suggested that social conflict played a negative role primarily by inducing macroeconomic mismanagement. The evidence also suggested that ethnic cleavages mattered to the ability to manage shocks, even when the quality of institutions is controlled for.

The research cited earlier, as well as that of other scholars, suggests the channels or mechanisms via which ethnic diversity and the resulting ethnic competition and strife are presumed to impact economic growth via self-serving policies (macro instability, financial repression, exchange rate overvaluation), retardation of appropriate public expenditures, ethnic nepotism, corruption, low tax compliance and hence public sector investments and low trust and hence high transaction costs.

Other scholars have refined and tweaked the empirics or come up with alternative and updated estimates of fragmentation but essentially supported the Easterly and Levine findings. Collier (2002) found that the negative impact of ethnic fragmentation on economic growth is more likely in societies with limited political rights. Corstange (2004) argued that interacting institutions with the ethnic fragmentation variable produced more convincing results, that is, the impact of ethnic fragmentation on economic growth was mediated via the nature of institutions. Posner (2004) challenged the basic measure of ethnic fragmentation being used by most scholars since it was dated,[12] groups ill-defined and not necessarily players. Based on a reconstruction of the ethnic fragmentation variable, the result that the latter negatively impacted economic growth mediated by poor choice of policies was replicated for 42 sub-Saharan African countries.[13]

Montalvo and Reynal-Querol (2005) explored the available data sources for measures of religious and ethnolinguistic fragmentation and polarization and followed that with empirical analysis on their impact on growth and development. On the one hand, they found that ethnolinguistic fragmentation had a direct negative impact on growth rather than via various channels, such as of a reduction of investment due to the enhanced probability of civil war or via greater rent-seeking activities. On the other hand, they found that ethnic polarization also reduced economic growth via the channels of reduced investment rate, enhanced consumption and incidence of civil war.

Easterly et al. (2006) showed that the impact of the lack of social cohesion (high inequality and fragmentation) was mediated via poor institutions (lack of rule of law, accountability, civil liberties and corruption).[14] Higher social cohesion resulted in better institutions that, in turn, lead to higher economic growth.

Alesina et al. (2011) directly addressed the research question of this book. They hypothesized that artificial (constructed) states perform less well than non-artificial (natural) ones in terms of indicators of economic and political development, education, health, public goods delivery, political instability and violence. They constructed two measures of artificiality. The first is the degree to which ethnic groups were split by borders by colonial powers. The second measure, in a nutshell, is how straight land borders are, under the assumption that straight borders are more like to be artificial and less likely to follow geographic features or the evolution of hundreds of years of border design. While the main contribution of the paper was purported to be measures of the artificiality of nations, the use to which this contribution is put is to show how these measures of artificiality are negatively associated with political and economic development of post-colonial independent states. In particular, they found a robust negative association of artificial states with per capita GDP growth controlling for a host of other relevant variables.

This finding was superseded by Alesina et al. (2016), who showed that the significance of ethnolinguistic fragmentation receded once cross ethnic (horizontal) inequality entered the equation. Thus, it was the unequal concentration of wealth across ethnicities rather than ethnic diversity per se that was inversely associated with development. In the same vein, Kyriacou (2013) found that ethnic group inequality had a negative impact on an aggregate indicator of governance including variables measuring corruption, the strength of law and order and the independence and effectiveness of public administration.

Apart from inducing a brain drain and the obvious destruction of infrastructure, Costalli et al. (2017) argued that civil war brought on by ethic fractionalization eroded inter-ethnic trust and hence business relations. Further, they argued that estimating the economic cost of civil wars is complex since getting appropriate counterfactuals is difficult due to endogeneity problems (civil war and poor performance are interrelated). The available options, before and after studies or comparisons with peaceful countries, were not deemed to be satisfactory. To address these problems, the authors used a synthetic control method to construct appropriate counterfactuals and measure the economic impact of civil war. They focused on the years of armed conflict in a sample of 20 countries and observed an average annual loss of local gross domestic product (GDP) per capita of 17.5 percent. The more fractionalized a country, the larger its economic losses.

While much of the research focus of economists has understandably been on the negative association of ethnic fragmentation and polarization on economic growth, social scientists have also demonstrated the negative association on broader development outcomes. For example, Easterly and Levine (1997), Alesina et al. (2003) and Montalvo and Reynal-Querol

(2005) pointed to lower levels of schooling and literacy; Easterly and Levine (1997) and Alesina et al. (2003), among others, have pointed to quality and quantity of public goods provision and social spending and transfers, higher infant mortality and less effective governance and so higher corruption. The significance level of these variables decreased controlling for per capita income.

Gershman and Rivera (2018) constructed a dataset based on population censuses and large-scale household surveys. They extracted information on regional ethnolinguistic composition in 36 countries and almost 400 first-level administrative units in sub-Saharan Africa. The dataset was utilized to examine the association between regional diversity and various development indicators, with a particular focus on schooling, health facilities and electricity. They found that only deep-rooted diversity, based on relatedness of language pairing, was inversely associated with schooling, health and electricity access. The negative association did not carry over to regional measures of income per capita and household wealth, and they emphasized, therefore, on the importance of a narrower focus on various development indicators in studies of ethnic diversity.

Finally, Pleninger and Sturm (2020) found a strongly negative association of de jure (not de facto) financial globalization on redistribution in highly fractionalized countries. The association was statistically insignificant for more ethnically homogenous countries. The authors speculated that there was a general unwillingness to compensate with policy for the perceived negative impact of financial globalization on inequality without generalized support for such action.

While this section has relied on reviewing the results of quantitative empirical studies, it needs to be noted that scholars who engage in cross-country empirical work generally qualify their results by pointing to limitations embodied in the empirical work they conducted based on measurement problems (of variables used) or the innate limitations of the empirical analysis. Other scholars have pointed to the much more serious limitation of cross-country analysis that lumps together countries at very different stages of economic development with very different structural features.[15]

Conclusion

This chapter starts by reviewing the evidence that constructed nations, with an amalgamation of ethnicities, are much more prone to social conflict that undermines their social and economic development. Next, the cross-country empirical evidence is reviewed, and this suggests for the most part that ethnic diversity and competition undermine social and economic development via various mechanisms, such as poor governance, corruption and poor policy selection.

Appendix Table 3.1a Ethnicity and ethnic conflict/civil war in low-income countries (LICs)

Low-income countries (<$1,085)	Number of ethnic groups (>2% of population)	Size of largest group (%)	Ethnic conflict/ civil war
Afghanistan	7	42	yes
Burkina Faso	10	52	yes
Burundi	2	85	yes
Central African Republic	9	29	yes
Chad	14	31	yes
Congo, Democratic Republic	4	48	yes
Eritrea	8	50	no
Ethiopia	8	36	yes
Gambia, The	6	33	yes
Guinea	5	33	yes
Guinea-Bissau	5	30	yes
Korea, DPR	1	100	no
Liberia	13	20	yes
Madagascar	20	24	yes
Malawi	8	33	no
Mali	5	50	yes
Mozambique	8	33	yes
Niger	5	55	yes*
Rwanda	2	84	yes
Sierra-Leone	6	35	yes
Somalia	1 plus	85	yes
South Sudan	20	35–40	yes
Sudan	4	90	yes
Syrian Arab Republic	4	50	yes
Togo	5	42	yes
Uganda	10	17	yes
Yemen, Republic	2	93	yes&
Zambia	15	21	no

Source: Country income group classification is based on the July 1, 2022, World Bank definition.

Data on national ethnicity are drawn mainly from CIA Factbook. Other sources consulted include World Atlas, Encyclopedia Britannica and www.nationmaster.com/country-info/stats/People/Ethnic-groups (consulted July 2022). Data on ethnic conflict and civil wars are drawn from numerous sources generated by Google searches.

Appendix Table 3.1b Ethnicity and ethnic conflict/civil war in (LMICs)

Low-middle income countries ($1,086–$4,255)	Number of ethnic groups (>2% of population)	Size of largest group (%)	Ethnic conflict/ civil war
Angola	4	37	yes
Algeria	1	99	yes
Bangladesh	1	98	no
Benin	8	38	yes
Bhutan	2	50	yes
Bolivia	4	30!	yes

Low-middle income countries ($1,086–$4,255)	Number of ethnic groups (>2% of population)	Size of largest group (%)	Ethnic conflict/ civil war
Cabo Verde	2	71	no
Cambodia	2	95	yes
Cameroon	9	24	yes
Comoros	5	86	yes
Congo, Republic	7	41	yes
Cote d'Ivoire	5	29	yes
Djibouti	2	60	yes
Egypt, Arab Republic	1 plus	98	yes
El Salvador	2	86	yes
Eswatini	2	84	no
Ghana	8	46	yes
Haiti	2	95	no
Honduras	3	90	no
India	2	72	yes
Indonesia	9	40	yes
Iran, Islamic Republic	7	61	yes
Kenya	11	17	yes
Kiribati	2	96	no
Kyrgyz Republic	3	74	yes
Lao, PDR	9	53	yes
Lebanon	2	95	yes
Lesotho	1 plus	98	no
Mauritania	3	40	yes
Micronesia, Federated States	5	49	no
Mongolia	4	84	no
Morocco	1 plus	99	yes
Myanmar	7	68	yes
Nepal	10	17	yes[@]
Nicaragua	4	69	yes
Nigeria	8	30	yes
Pakistan	6	45	yes
Papua New Guinea	5	na	yes
Philippines	7	24	yes
Samoa	2	96	no
Sao Tome and Principe	4	80	no
Senegal	5	43	yes
Soloman Islands	2	95	yes
Sri Lanka	4	75	yes
Tanzania	1 plus[#]	95	yes^
Tajikistan	2	80	yes
Timor-Leste	3	na	yes
Tunisia	1 plus	98	yes
Ukraine	2	78	yes
Uzbekistan	5	84	yes
Vanuatu	1 plus	99	no

(*Continued*)

Appendix Table 3.1b (Continued)

Low-middle income countries ($1,086–$4,255)	Number of ethnic groups (>2% of population)	Size of largest group (%)	Ethnic conflict/ civil war
Vietnam	3	85	yes
West Bank and Gaza	2	83	yes
Zimbabwe	2	82	yes

Source: See Appendix Table 3.1a.

Notes:
na = Not available
@ = Ideological conflict
# = The ethnic group is Bantu, but there are over 130 tribes
^ = Notably less so than other sub-Saharan African countries
! = There are considerable differences in reported ethnic composition in different sources

Appendix Table 3.1c Ethnicity and ethnic conflict/civil war in (HMICs)

Upper-middle income countries ($4,265–$13,205)	Number of ethnic groups (>2% of population)	Size of largest group (%)	Ethnic conflict/ civil war
Albania	1 plus	82	yes
American Samoa	4	90	no
Argentina	2	97	no
Armenia	1 plus	98	no
Azerbaijan	2	92	no
Belarus	4	84	no
Belize	6	53	no
Bosnia and Herzegovina	3	50	yes
Botswana	3	79	no
Brazil	3	48	no[&]
Bulgaria	3	77	no[+]
China	1 plus	91	yes
Costa Rica	3	84	no[!]
Cuba	3	64	no[!]
Dominica	4	85	no
Dominican Republic	3	70	no
Equatorial Guinea	4	86	yes
Ecuador	6	72	yes
Fiji	2	57	yes
Gabon	12	23	no
Georgia	3	87	yes
Grenada	3	82	no
Guatemala	3	56	yes
Guyana	4	40	yes
Iraq	2	75–80	yes
Jamaica	2	92	no[@]
Jordan	4	69	no
Kazakhstan	4	68	yes
Kosovo	3	93	no
Libya	1 plus	97	yes

Upper-middle income countries ($4,265–$13,205)	Number of ethnic groups (>2% of population)	Size of largest group (%)	Ethnic conflict/ civil war
Malaysia	3	63	yes
Maldives	1 plus	99	no⁻
Marshall Islands	2	92	no
Mauritius	4	68	yes
Mexico	3	62	yes
Moldova	6	75	yes
Montenegro	5	45	no⁺
Namibia	10	50	no
North Macedonia	4	58	yes
Palau	3	73	no
Paraguay	1 plus	95	no
Peru	4	60	yes
Russian Federation	2	78	yes
Serbia	4	83	no
South Africa	4	81	no[%]
Saint Lucia	4	85	no
St. Vincent and the Grenadines	3	71	no
Suriname	5	27	yes
Thailand	1 plus	98	yes
Tonga	1 plus	97	no
Türkiye	2	70–75	yes
Turkmenistan	3	85	no[#]
Tuvalu	1 plus	97	no

Source: See Appendix Table 3.1a.

Notes:
& = Racial tension has been on the rise
+ = There have been ethnic tensions
! = Racism remains an issue
@ = Ideological violence
~ = Political tension
% = Anti-immigrant and anti-poverty violence
# = Country noted for authoritarianism and oppression of minorities

Notes

1 The World Bank classifies countries based on per capita gross national income into low, low middle, upper middle and high income. Refer to Appendix Tables 3.1(a–c) for the income classifications.
2 Refer to Bangura (2006) for case studies based on an elaborate typology of ethnic diversity, including unipolar, bipolar, tripolar, concentrated multipolar and fragmented multipolar.
3 For literature reviews on ethnicity and conflict, refer to Vorrath and Krebs (2009), Hillesund et al. (2018) and Kanbur et al. (2011) for a multidisciplinary perspective. With qualifications, the consensus in all these studies is of a positive association of ethnicity and conflict, including armed conflict. Also refer to Blattman and Miguel (2010) on the broader theme of civil wars. Citing (Fearon, 2006), they point out that of 709 minority ethnic groups identified around the world, at least 100 had members engaged in an ethnically based rebellion against the state during 1945–1998. Refer to Stewart (2000) for an exposition of horizontal inequalities, including among ethnic groups and policy suggestions for conflict prevention.

4 Houle and Bodea (2017) used group-level data for 32 sub-Saharan African countries and 141 ethnic groups between 1960 and 2005 to explore the association of ethnic inequality on coups. They found strong support for their hypothesis that between-ethnic-group inequality increases the likelihood that an ethnic group stages a coup when within ethnic-group inequality is low.

5 Scholars distinguish between ethnic fragmentation (fractionalization) and polarization. Indices for the latter measure the extent to which the ethnic composition of a society is bipolar.

6 Ethnic conflict or civil war here only refers to those that take place within the borders of the country in question. So, for example, cross-border ethnic conflict between Armenians and Azeris is not included as ethnic conflict in Appendix Tables 3.1(a–c). Also, ethnic tensions that do not rise to overt discord and bloodshed, such as that between the Bulgarians and Turks in Bulgaria, are not noted as conflict.

7 Note that small island nations, sometimes with a population less than 100,000, have not been excluded as is often done in such research.

8 For a review of the early literature, refer to Alesina and La Ferrara (2005), who also reviewed studies conducted at the micro level.

9 Much of this literature was devoted to explaining the so-called African Tragedy identified by Easterly and Levine (1997). Ironically, other scholars were observing "Africa Rising" in the 1990s and on into the first two decades of the twenty-first century. For example, the World Bank noted that six among the ten fastest-growing economies in the first decade of the twenty-first century were African. Both generalizations miss the vast variation in the continent as noted by Radalet (2016).

10 Insofar as authors who focused on the negative impact of ethnic diversity provided suggestions on how to address problems of ethnic diversity and induce national cohesion, these suggestions are discussed in Chapter 5.

11 As Green (2019) described in simple terms, a country's ethnolinguistic fragmentation score is calculated using the Herfindahl concentration formula. This requires summing the squares of the percentages of all ethnic groups, larger than 1 percent of the population, and subtracting this sum from one. Thus, in the limit if one group represents 100 percent of the population, the fragmentation score would be zero, and so the greater the fragmentation, the higher the score.

12 Most of the early measures of ethnic fragmentation were based on Atlas Narodov Mira (Atlas of Peoples of the World, 1964).

13 Other scholars who have replicated the negative association of economic growth with ethnic fragmentation include Schneider and Wiesehomeier (2009) and Wunnava et al. (2015).

14 In a similar vein, Hanson (2013) showed that the impact of ethnic diversity on education and health was mediated via geography, especially how concentrated or dispersed ethnicities were in a particular region in a country.

15 Refer to Fine (2001, pp. 141–143) for a critique. Levine and Zervos (1993) also identify the many statistical and conceptual problems of cross-country regressions such as shortcomings of the data and measurement problems for L/LMICs, in particular, and lumping together vastly different countries, hence implicitly assuming a structural similarity that does not exist. Further, the pooling of cross section and time series data ignores political changes and business cycles among many other relevant phenomena not captured. Finally, they do not represent behavioral associations, are unable to measure the impact of executable policy, given the nature of the data, and do not represent causal associations. Nonetheless, Levine and Zervos were not entirely dismissive and proposed a test to identify robust associations between variables in question. As several of the articles cited in the references show, the econometrics has become more sophisticated over time in the use of instrumental variables and other methods for coming closer in identifying causal associations and robust coefficients. However, the underlying conceptual and measurement problems remain, and at best, the results of the sophisticated econometrics are suggestive.

References

Alesina, A., Devleeschauwer, A., Easterly, W., Kurlat, S. and Wacziarg, R. 2003. 'Fractionalization', *Journal of Economic Growth*, 8(2), 155–194.

Alesina, A. and La Ferrara, E. 2005. 'Ethnic diversity and economic performance',
Journal of Economic Literature, 43(3), 762–800.

Alesina, A., Matuszeski, J. and Easterly, W. 2011. 'Artificial States', *Journal of the
European Economic Association*, 9(2), 246–277.

Alesina, A., Michalopoulos, S. and Papaioannou, E. 2016. 'Ethnic inequality', *Journal
of Political Economy*, 124(2), 428–488.

Atlas Narodov Mira. 1964. Moscow: Miklukho-Maklai Ethno-logical Institute, Department of Geodesy and Cartography, State Geological Committee of the Soviet Union.

Bang, J.T. and Mitra, A. 2013. 'Civil war, ethnicity, and the migration of skilled labor',
Eastern Economic Journal, 39(3), 387–401.

Bangura, Y. 2006. 'Ethnic inequalities in the public sector: A comparative analysis',
Development and Change, 37(2), 299–328.

Bates, R. H. 1999. 'Ethnicity, capital formation, and conflict', Center for International
Development Working Paper No. 27, Harvard University, Cambridge, MA.

Blattman, C. and Miguel, E. 2010. 'Civil war', *Journal of Economic Literature*, 48(1), 3–57.

Bosker, M. and de Ree, J. 2014. 'Ethnicity and the spread of civil war', *Journal of
Development* Economics, 108(C), 206–221.

Canelasa, C. and Gisselquist, R.M. 2018. 'Horizontal inequality as an outcome', *Oxford
Development Studies*, 46(3), 305–324.

Collier, P. 2002. 'Ethnicity, politics and economic performance', *Economics and Politics*, 12(3), 225–245.

Corstange, D. 2004. 'New findings on the effects of ethnic divisions on African Economic Growth', Paper prepared for presentation at the 2004 conference of the Midwest Political Science Association, Chicago, IL.

Costalli, S., Moretti, L. and Pischedda, C. 2017. 'The economic costs of civil war: Synthetic counterfactual evidence and the effects of ethnic fractionalization', *Journal of
Peace Research*, 54(1), 80–89.

Deiwiks, C., Cederman, L.-E. and Gleditsch, K.S. 2012. 'Inequality and conflict in
federations', *Journal of Peace Research*, 49(2), 289–304.

Easterly, W. and Levine, R. 1997. 'Africa's growth tragedy: Policies and ethnic divisions', *The Quarterly Journal of Economics*, 112(4), 1203–1250.

Easterly, W., Ritzen, J. and Woolcock, M. 2006. 'Social cohesion, institution and
growth', *Journal of Economics and Politics*, 18(2), 102–120.

Esteban, J., Mayoral, L. and Ray, D. 2012. 'Ethnicity and conflict: An empirical study',
The American Economic Review, 102(4), 1310–1342.

Fearon, J.D. 2006. 'Ethnic mobilization and ethnic violence', in Weingast, B.R. and
Wittman, D.A. (eds.) *The Oxford handbook of political economy*. Oxford: Oxford
University Press, 852–868.

Fine, B. 2001. 'The social capital of the World Bank', in Fine, B., Lapavistsas, C. and
Pincus, J. (eds.) *Development policy in the twenty-first century: Beyond the post-
Washington consensus*. London: Routledge.

Gershman, B. and Rivera, D. 2018. 'Subnational diversity in Sub-Saharan Africa: Insights
from a new dataset', *Journal of Development Economics*, 133(July), 231–263.

Green, E. 2019. 'Industrialization and ethnic change in the modern world', *Ethnic and
Racial Studies*, 42(2), 178–197.

Hanson, J.K. 2013. 'Diversity and development: The interaction of political institutions with social context', Prepared for presentation at the 2013 Annual Meeting of the Midwest Political Science Association, April 11–14.

Hillesund, S., et al. 2018. 'Horizontal inequality and armed conflict: A comprehensive literature review', *Canadian Journal of Development Studies*, 39(4), 463–480.

Houle, C. and Bodea, C. 2017. 'Ethnic inequality and coups in sub-Saharan Africa', *Journal of Peace Research*, 54(3), 382–396.

Kanbur, R., Rajaram, P.K. and Varshney, A. 2011. 'Ethnic diversity and ethnic strife. An interdisciplinary perspective', *World Development*, 39(2), 147–158.

Kyriacou, A.P. 2013. 'Ethnic group inequalities and governance: Evidence from developing countries', *Kyklos*, 66(1), 78–101.

Langer, A., Stewart, F., Smedts, K. and Demarest, L. 2017. 'Conceptualizing and measuring social cohesion in Africa: Towards a perceptions-based index', *Social Indicators Research*, 131, 321–343.

Levine, R. and Zervos, S.J. 1993. 'What we have learned about policy and growth from cross-country regressions?', *The American Economic Review*, 83(2), 426–430.

Montalvo, J.G. and Reynal-Querol, M. 2005. 'Ethnic diversity and economic development', *Journal of Development Economics*, 76(2), 293–323.

Montalvo, J.G. and Reynal-Querol, M. 2020. 'Ethnic diversity and growth: Revisiting the evidence', Barcelona GSE Working Paper Series Working Paper No. 992E. Barcelona School of Economics, Barcelona.

Østby, G. 2008. 'Polarization, horizontal inequalities and violent civil conflict', *Journal of Peace Research*, 45(2), 143–62.

Pleninger, R. and Sturm, J.-E. 2020. 'The effects of economic globalisation and ethnic fractionalisation on redistribution', *World Development*, 130, 1–19.

Posner, D.N. 2004. 'Measuring ethnic fractionalization in Africa', *American Journal of Political Science*, 48(4), 849–863.

Radalet, S. 2016. 'Africa's rise – interrupted?', *Finance and Development*, 53(2), 6–10.

Repkine, A. 2014. 'Ethnic diversity, political stability and productive efficiency: Empirical evidence from the African countries', *South African Journal of Economics*, 82(3), 315–333.

Rodrik, D. 1999. 'Where did all the growth go? External shocks, social conflict, and growth collapses', *Journal of Economic Growth*, 4(4), 385–412.

Schneider, G. and Wiesehomeier, N. 2009. 'Diversity, conflict and growth: Theory and evidence', *Diversity*, 2010, 2(9), 1097–1117.

Stewart, F. 2000. 'Crisis prevention: Tackling horizontal inequalities', *Oxford Development Studies*, 28(3), 245–262.

Vorrath, J. and Krebs, L.F. 2009. 'Democratisation and conflict in ethnically divided societies', *Living Reviews in Democracy*, 1(1), 1–9.

Wegenast, T.C. and Basedau, M. 2014. 'Ethnic fractionalization, natural resources and armed conflict', *Conflict Management and Peace Science*, 31(4), 432–457.

Wunnava, P.V., Mitra, A. and Prasch, R.E. 2015. 'Globalization and the ethnic divide: Recent longitudinal evidence', *Social Science Quarterly*, 96(5), 1475–1492.

4 Independence, ethnicity and development

Case studies

Introduction

This chapter focuses on two related stories. The overarching story is that of the independence of nations in a changed geography. The contention is that the morale boost and national drive that are likely to accompany independence can enhance economic and social development. The related story is that of ethnic homogeneity and how that might enhance economic development (see Chapter 3 for a literature review).

This chapter first considers a comparative case study, which comes close to a natural experiment, that is, the comparison between Bangladesh and Pakistan.[1] The second comparative case study is an exploration of how independence may have impacted the Balkan nations born after the collapse of the Soviet Union. While independence may have accompanied the changed geography, only half of the eight Balkan countries that declared independence after the collapse of the Soviet Union could be considered natural nations (with a dominant ethnicity of around 90 percent or more). This provides the opportunity to explore the impact of independence, even if it is not accompanied by the national cohesion that might accompany being a natural nation.

A comprehensive historical analysis is needed to understand the current state of play in each country. That task and how ethnicity historically played a role in shaping a nation's destiny, natural or constructed, is left to other scholars. The hope is that the analysis in this and the following chapter will whet the appetite of scholars to engage in a more comprehensive analysis.

Bangladesh and Pakistan[2]

The ethnic profiles of Bangladesh and Pakistan are presented in Table 4.1.

Based on the working definition of natural nations used in this book, Bangladesh fits the bill with 98 percent of the population being of Bengali ethnicity. Pakistan, a typical colonial constructed nation, by contrast, has six notable (2 percent or more of the population) ethnicities. Punjabis, as the predominant ethnicity, have much of the political power and dominate the military and

DOI: 10.4324/9781032630878-4

Table 4.1 Ethnic profiles of Bangladesh and Pakistan (% distribution)

Bangladesh	%	Pakistan	%
Bengali	98.0	Punjabi	44.8
Other	2.0	Pathan	15.4
		Sindhi	14.1
		Saraiki	8.4
		Muhajir	7.4
		Balochi	3.6
		Other	6.3

Source: www.nationmaster.com/country-info/stats/People/Ethnic-groups, gathered from Country Censuses, consulted March 31, 2022.

bureaucracy. It shares power positions with the Pashtuns (Pathans), the second-most populous ethnicity, but one with only about a third of the population of Punjabis. The British viewed the Punjabis and Pathans as martial races and actively recruited them for the British Indian army, and the tradition continued even after independence.[3]

Just as the East Pakistanis essentially viewed the Punjabis as the oppressors, almost all the other ethnicities within what was West Pakistan (now Pakistan) have sought separation from the Punjab. The Punjabis are viewed as the ruling ethnic group because of their hold on military, civil, political and economic power.

The followers of Khan Abdul Ghaffar Khan (the Khudai Khidmatgars) sought Pashtunistan to unite Pushto-speaking peoples in Pakistan and Afghanistan in the first few decades after the birth of the country. However, having secured the name Khyber-Pakhtunkhwa in 2010, after a long political struggle, and having acquired significant influence in the military, bureaucracy and politics, the Pashtuns in Pakistan appear contented for now in the Pakistani fold.[4] They may also have thought twice about hitching their wagon to a troubled Afghanistan.

There are several separatist groups in Sindh seeking a Sindhudesh, though a leading English language daily reported in March 2022 that many of them, represented by over 200 leaders, decided to quit separatism to join national politics.[5] The alleged reason was the hesitancy of local Sindhi leaders in accepting foreign funding and being guided by expatriates living comfortable lives abroad while pushing their agendas in Pakistan. One of the key political parties in the country, the Pakistan People's Party (PPP, formed in 1967), was founded by a Sindhi politician and continues to dominate Sindhi politics. It also has a national presence and has been in power several times, and this may have appeased Sindhi nationalism to some extent.

Foreign funding is also alleged to be pushing an ongoing separatism in Balochistan, though several of the leaders are willing to settle for a fair share of its rich natural resources for the Balochi people.[6] A low-level insurgency is ongoing with the military trying to repress it. Insurgencies tend to pick up during military dictatorships when high-handed trampling of rights is more evident, while, in general, political regimes are more willing to engage and compromise (Chapter 5).

Many of the Urdu-speaking Muhajirs in the Sindh province are the descendants of those who migrated from India and are widely viewed as having contributed greatly to stabilizing the newly independent country. Initially they were well represented in the central bureaucracy and in urban Sindh, mainly Karachi city, the foremost financial, commercial and industrial hub and the key port of the country. As the Sindhis in rural Sindh gained political power, even at the national level, governance in Karachi was contested, and the displacement of the Muhajirs resulted in their disaffection, and Muhajir militant groups emerged, belying the popular myth of them being pushovers, and made Karachi ungovernable for a while.

Three ethnic groups have not manifested separatism. The Saraiki people are dominant in southern Punjab and have pushed for a separate province (Saraikistan) between Punjab and Sindh. It constitutes just over half the land area and about a third of the population of the Punjab. Mainstream Punjabi politicians have opposed the dilution of the province's political and economic power, but the administration of the Pakistan Tehreek-e-Insaaf (PTI, 2019–2022), whose primary base was Khyber-Pakhtunkhwa, won many seats in the National Assembly from southern Punjab, by promising the creation of a separate province. The PPP has, for obvious political reasons, also supported the creation of Saraikistan. In 2022, the Senate (upper house) passed a bill supporting the creation of a Saraikistan as a separate province, and, while a separate administrative secretariat has been established, Saraikistan is not yet a full-fledged province.

Similarly, the predominantly Hindko-speaking Hindkowan people of Hazarajat region in Khyber-Pakhtunkhwa province have clamored for a separate province, and this gained speed after the North-West Frontier Province was renamed Khyber-Pakhtunkhwa in 2010. The political demand to name Hazara division a separate province is ongoing.[7]

The Kashmiris are not shown as an ethnic group in Table 4.1 because Kashmir remains a contested territory since 1948. In Pakistan-administered Kashmir, there has been no separatism to date. However, the Kashmiris in the Pakistan-administered Kashmir resent the limited representation and empowerment granted to them constitutionally, while a definitive UN resolution of the conflict is being (indefinitely) awaited. For example, the AJ&K Interim Constitution Act, 1974, that provides governance powers to "local authority" grants very limited autonomy and no representation in Parliament or constitutional bodies (Gardezi et al., 2015).

Pakistan's ethnic mix, as expected, complicates the politics.[8] That notwithstanding, Pakistan has ironically made progress toward national cohesion under political regimes that recognized the importance of moving to a federation by recognizing provinces (rather than treating Pakistan as one unit as was the case with West Pakistan) and granting more provincial autonomy over time (Chapter 5). However, the complicated politics due to ethnic diversity and the instability it creates result in economic setbacks and have also created opportunities for the military to seize power several times.

The question of interest for this chapter is how Bangladesh, with its ethnic unity, fared in social and economic terms relative to the ethnically diverse Pakistan after gaining independence in 1971. The latter year is used as the base year for comparison, and 2021, the latest year for which data were available from the World Bank's World Development Indicators, is used as the terminal year. The comparative development statistics are presented in Table 4.2.

Table 4.2 makes clear that Bangladesh has outpaced Pakistan in all social and economic indicators. Except for foreign currency (FOREX) reserves, Pakistan was ahead of Bangladesh on all the selected indicators in the base

Table 4.2 Indicators of progress: Bangladesh and Pakistan

Indicator	Bangladesh		Pakistan	
	1971	*2020*	*1971*	*2020*
Access to electricity (% of population)	26.7[@]	96.2	70.5[@]	75.4
Fixed broadband subscriptions (per 100 people)	na	6.1	na	1.1
Gross domestic product (GDP) per capita (constant 2015 US$)	474.5	1715.4[!]	576.0	1,507.1[!]
Industry (including construction), value added (% of GDP)	7.7	33.3[!]	15.2	12.0[!]
Present value of external debt (% of gross national income [GNI])	na	13.0	na	30.3
Total reserves (% of total external debt)	28.7[^]	63.4	12.9[^]	15.9
Total reserves in months of imports	3.5[#]	6.3[!]	10.1[#]	3.4[!]
Human Development Index	0.39	0.63	0.40	0.56

Source: World Development Indicators, update June 30, 2022.

https://hdr.undp.org/data-center/human-development-index#/indicies/HDI for the Human Development Index.

Notes:
na = not applicable or not available
[!] = For 2021
[@] = For 1998
[#] = For 1976
[^] = For 1972
The base year for the Human Development Index is 1990, and the terminal year is 2019.

years. However, in the terminal years, Bangladesh outperformed Pakistan in all the selected indicators.

Per capita gross domestic product (GDP) in 1971 (in constant 2015 $s) was 12 percent higher in Pakistan, but by 2021, it was 14 percent higher in Bangladesh, and the gap is likely to continue to grow given the much higher growth trajectory in Bangladesh.[9] Access to electricity in Bangladesh increased from 27 percent in 1998 to 96 percent of the population in 2020, while in Pakistan, it remained virtually stationary (an increase from 71 percent to 74 percent). Industrialization in Bangladesh increased more than fourfold between 1971 and 2021 (industrial value added as a percent of GDP increased from 7.7 percent to 33.3 percent). Pakistan, by comparison, deindustrialized such that its industrial value added in the same period decreased from 15 percent (twice that of Bangladesh in 1971) to 12 percent in 2021. Bangladesh is the only country in South Asia, and in much of the developing world, that has avoided premature deindustrialization (Rodrik, 2015) and even held its own against the onslaught of competition from China, particularly in the textiles and garment industry.

Other indicators similarly reveal a superior performance for Bangladesh. A far lower level of indebtedness and much higher FOREX reserves suggest superior economic management and a much more sustainable economy than crisis-ridden Pakistan. In 1971, the Bangladeshi taka was valued at 21 to US$1, and by April 2023, it had depreciated to 106 takas to US$1. Over the same time period, the Pakistani rupee depreciated from Rs. 9 to Rs. 280 to a dollar.

Bangladesh's present value of external debt as a percentage of gross national income (GNI) in 2020 was 13 percent compared to Pakistan's 30 percent. Its FOREX reserves as a percentage of total external debt increased from 29 percent in 1972 to 63 percent in 2020, while Pakistan's corresponding reserves increased from 13 percent to 16 percent. In terms of months of imports, Bangladesh's reserves increased from three months of imports in 1976 to about twice that in 2021. For the corresponding years, Pakistan's reserves declined from ten months to three months.

It is not surprising then that Pakistan has sought assistance from the International Monetary Fund (IMF) a total of 23 times – the last program approval at the time of writing was June 2023. By contrast, Bangladesh sought IMF's assistance ten times, most in the first two decades of its independence and the last one in 2012.[10] Over the last decade (2012–2022), its solid economic management and performance, low debt and high reserves gave it a high measure of economic sovereignty, that is, it did not need the assistance of the IMF.[11]

Unlike other countries in the emerging world, Bangladesh's catch-up growth has not been accompanied by a rise in inequality. Its Gini coefficient of 32 in 2016 was the lowest in South Asia, and its human development indicators made a great stride from 0.39 in 1971 to 0.63 in 2020. Over the same period, Pakistan's Human Development Index increased from 0.40 to 0.56, higher only than Afghanistan in South Asia.

Table 4.3 Comparative governance indicators for Bangladesh and Pakistan: percentile rank

Indicator	Bangladesh		Pakistan	
	Average 1996–2021	*2021*	*Average 1996–2021*	*2021*
Control of corruption	14.1 (7.6)	18.3	18.7 (4.7)	23.6
Voice and accountability	33.8 (6.2)	28.01	24.0 (5.0)	25.1
Rule of law	23.3 (4.8)	28.8	23.3 (3.6)	28.0
Regulatory quality	18.1 (2.6)	20.7	26.9 (4.0)	26.0
Government effectiveness	24.9 (3.9)	28.8	31.1 (5.9)	28.8

Source: Worldwide Governance Indicators, last updated September 23, 2022.

Notes: Parentheses contain standard deviations.

Tables 4.3 and 4.4 explore the importance of political and economic governance institutions in contributing to Bangladesh's success relative to Pakistan as noted earlier.

Table 4.3 provides data on five political governance indicators that include control of corruption, voice and accountability, rule of law, regulatory quality and government effectiveness. Looking at averages over the 1996–2021 period, Pakistan ranks notably better than Bangladesh on control of corruption, regulatory quality and government effectiveness. The ranks are identical, though low, for rule of law, and Bangladesh ranks higher for voice and accountability.

Table 4.4 provides data on economic governance indicators.

Pakistan outranked Bangladesh on all except for one indicator: it took about the same senior management time dealing with government regulatory requirements in Pakistan as in Bangladesh in 2013, the latest year for which this information is available at the time of writing. For most indicators, the time series starts in 2013, and Pakistan consistently improved on all indicators over time, while performance in Bangladesh was virtually stagnant across the board except in "time required to get electricity" and "ease of doing business".[12] Even for the latter indicator, Bangladesh's progress was from 41 in 2015 to 45 in 2019, while Pakistan progressed from 50 to 61.

The better political and economic governance statistics and their improvement over time in Pakistan provide a puzzle for researchers as to why they are not accompanied by improving social and economic performance as in Bangladesh. Referring back to the New Institutional Economics (NIE) narrative in Chapter 1, it can be argued that despite poor political and economic governance, ethnic homogeneity enabled the building of more inclusive institutions

Table 4.4 Comparative economic governance indicators for Bangladesh and Pakistan, 2019

Indicator	Bangladesh		Pakistan	
	Average 2013–2019	*2019*	*Average 2013–2019*	*2019*
Ease of doing business rank (1 = most business-friendly regulations)	na	168.0	na	108.0
Ease of doing business score (0 = lowest performance to 100 = best performance)	44.2!	45.0	54.5!	61.0
Time required to get electricity (days)	279.5	124.5	160.1	113.0
Time required to obtain an operating license (days) / 2013	na	33.5	na	10.4
Time required to start a business (days)	19.8	19.5	18.9	16.5
Time required to register property (days)	270.8	270.8	147.4	104.7
Time spent dealing with the requirements of government regulations (% of senior management time) / 2013	na	3.3	na	3.5
Time to export, border compliance (hours)	168.0	168.0	73.5	58.0
Time to export, documentary compliance (hours)	147.0	147.0	57.9	55.0
Time to import, border compliance (hours)	216	216	123.8	120.0
Time to import, documentary compliance (hours)	144	144	99.9	96.0
Time to resolve insolvency (years)	4.0	4.0	2.6	2.6

Source: Worldwide Governance Indicators, last updated September 23, 2022.

Notes: Parentheses contain standard deviations
na = Not available
! = Starting year for average is 2015

in Bangladesh as a natural nation relative to Pakistan as a constructed nation. This is evident in the rapid progress of human development indicators in Bangladesh relative to the very slow progress of these indicators in Pakistan.[13]

Military expenditure as a percentage of GDP is also where inclusiveness or the lack of it comes into play. The differential in military expenditure of 1.3 percent of GDP in Bangladesh relative to 3.8 percent of GDP in Pakistan in 2021 is telling.[14] One could argue that Pakistan needs higher military expenditure since it is confronted with hostile neighbors, particularly India. This is not self-evident. It can also be argued that the military (predominantly

Punjabi) has used the hostility to procure privileges and build a vast economic empire and that it has an interest in continued hostility to sustain its privileges as documented by Siddiqa (2007) and Khan et al. (2014). If the well-being of the citizens was of concern, the state would have invested in peace and hence in its own people as Bangladesh has done.[15]

While ethic homogeneity has likely played a role in Bangladesh's far superior social and economic performance after independence than that of Pakistan, as noted earlier, independence, per se, may have contributed to this performance. Another natural experiment to glean the importance of independence to overall development is provided by the Balkan nations that declared independence after the collapse of the Soviet Union since only half of the eight such nations could be considered natural nations.

The Balkans

The dissolution of the Soviet Union (1988–1991) had, and continues to have, far-reaching effects on the global political landscape. One of these effects was the declaration of independence by many Balkan countries. Table 4.5 shows that six of the eight did so between 1991 and 1992 and the remaining two, Montenegro and Kosovo, declared independence, respectively, in 2006 and 2008.

Two of the eight, Croatia and Kosovo, became natural nations by the definition being used in this book such that the majority ethnicity composed at least 90 percent of the population. Serbia and Slovenia followed close behind with the majority ethnicity constituting 83 percent of the population.

Table 4.6 tracks how these countries did economically and socially relative to the year they declared independence. Per capita GDP and the Human Development Index are used, respectively, as summary indicators of economic and

Table 4.5 Ethnic diversity in newly independent Balkan nations

Country	Number of ethnic groups (> 2% of population)	Size of largest group (%)	Date of formation	Ethnic conflict or tension
Bosnia and Herzegovina	3	50	March 1992	yes
Croatia	3	90	June 1991	no
Kosovo	3	93	February 2008	no
Moldova	6	75	August 1991	yes
Montenegro	5	45	May 2006	yes
North Macedonia	4	58	September 1991	yes
Serbia	4	83	March 1992	no
Slovenia	3	83	June 1991	no

Source: Data on national ethnicity are drawn mainly from CIA Factbook. Other sources consulted include World Atlas, Encyclopedia Britannica and www.nationmaster.com/country-info/stats/People/Ethnic-groups (consulted July 2022).

Table 4.6 Economic and social performance in newly independent Balkan nations

Country	Percentage growth in GDP per capita (constant 2015 US$) since independence	Period	Human Development Index growth since independence	Period
Bosnia and Herzegovina	845.6	1994–2021	14.7	1991–2019
Croatia	105.0	1995–2021	26.9	1991–2019
Kosovo	64.7	2008–2021	na	na
Moldova	150.0	1995–2021	5.7	1991–2019
Montenegro	63.5	1997–2021	7.8	1991–2019
North Macedonia	54.9	1991–2021	13.2	2000–2019
Serbia	86.1	1995–2021	12.5	1991–2019
Slovenia	155.9	1995–2021	19.5	1991–2019

Source: World Development Indicators, update June 30, 2022.

https://hdr.undp.org/data-center/human-development-index#/indicies/HDI for the Human Development Index (HDI).

social progress. Since country performance is being compared to their own starting point, the different initial conditions are not an issue. However, there is also an implicit difference in difference comparison that gleans the impact of ethnic diversity.

All the Balkan countries in Table 4.6 show spectacular growth in per capita GDP since independence. This occurred whether or not they are natural nations or have or have not experienced ethnic conflict or tensions. Gaining independence seems to have boosted economic performance, and becoming more integrated with the European Union, even if not formally (except for Slovenia and Croatia, the two most prosperous nations),[16] has certainly helped. The human development indicators also show solid though not spectacular improvements except for Croatia and Slovenia.

Another way of viewing the progress of the eight Balkan countries in the sample is in terms of country rankings in per capita GNI and the human development indicators by the World Bank and the United Nations Development Programme (UNDP), respectively. The results are reported in Table 4.7.

All the eight Balkan countries in the sample were classified as middle income in the respective base years for which data were available. All of them enhanced their income classification to upper middle income, except for Croatia and Slovenia, which moved to high-income status by 2021. Similarly, on the human development classifications, the four countries that were ranked as medium human development in the base years (Bosnia and Herzegovina, Croatia, Moldova and North Macedonia) moved to high human development status by 2019, expect for Croatia, which moved to very high human

Table 4.7 Per capita GDP and Human Development Index (HDI) status improvements of Balkan nations since independence

Country	Period	Per capita gross national income (GNI) in base year	Per capita gross domestic income (GDI) in terminal year	Period	HDI in base year	HDI in terminal year
Bosnia and Herzegovina	2003–2021	Middle	Upper middle	2003–2019	Medium	High
Croatia	1997–2021	Middle	High	1997–2019	Medium	Very high
Kosovo	2021	na	Upper middle	–	na	na
Moldova	1995–2021	Middle	Upper middle	1995–2019	Medium	High
Montenegro	2009–2021	Middle	Upper middle	2009–2019	High	Very high
North Macedonia	2002–2021	Middle	Upper middle	2002–2019	Medium	High
Serbia	2009–2021	Middle	Upper middle	2009–2019	High	Very high
Slovenia	1997–2021	Middle	High	1997–2019	High	Very high

Source: For 2021 per capita national income classifications in 2021, https://datahelpdesk. worldbank.org/knowledgebase/articles/906519-world-bank-country-and-lending-groups, consulted August 11, 2022. For the income classifications in the base years and for the human development classifications, *Human Development Reports*, various issues.

Notes:
na = not available

development status. The three countries in the high human development status in the base year (Montenegro, Serbia and Slovenia) also moved to the very high human development status by 2019. Thus, across the board, the social and economic progress across all the Balkan countries that declared independence after the breakup of the Soviet Union has been remarkable.

A more rigorous way to test if independence boosted economic output is to estimate if the per capita GDP series in constant 2015 $s and the per capita GDP series in constant 2017 purchasing power parity $s show a structural break after independence. Unfortunately, enough times series observations were only available to do the tests for Montenegro. The Chow test suggests a structural break in both series, that is, GDP was boosted after independence.[17]

Conclusion

This chapter explores two related themes. First, in keeping with the main theme of the book, Bangladesh's social and economic performance since independence is compared to that of Pakistan. While it lagged behind Pakistan in all selected social and economic indicators at the time of independence in 1971, by 2021, it outperformed Pakistan in all these indicators. Also, given its economic growth trajectory in the past two decades, it seemed well on its way to leaving Pakistan far behind in terms of the social and economic well-being of its citizens.

More important, its solid economic performance, low debt and strong reserves meant it acquired economic sovereignty in the first two decades of the twenty-first century and could follow, until recently, its own path to social and economic progress without having to follow the dictates of the IMF. Meanwhile, in July 2019, Pakistan entered its 23rd IMF agreement since 1950.

It is very likely that ethnic homogeneity of Bangladesh (98 percent Bengali) had something to do with its national cohesion and social and economic progress. It's much greater investment in its own population, and hence, the much greater progress in human development indicators harkens back to the NIE building of inclusive institutions, as narrated in Chapter 1. It also harkens back to conceptual framework of a collective will to develop, as explicated in Chapter 2. Also, since the beneficiaries are more likely to be "people like us" rather than "the other", the political and civil society leadership is more willing to invest in its own people.

However, even with ethnic homogeneity within Bangladesh, other sources of conflict are evident. Just as in high-income countries (HICs), political divisions have emerged. In the current phase in Bangladesh's history, divisions are based on an overlay of religious ideology and politics. Humans appear to have a propensity for conflict, so the best one can hope for is that as institutions and politics mature, differences do not result in violent conflict. As the January 6, 2021, assault on the US Congress suggests, political maturity is not necessarily linear.

It is also likely that the high morale and national drive accompanying independence boosted Bangladesh's social and economic performance. The social and economic performance of the Balkan nations, which declared independence since the collapse of the Soviet Union, was explored and found to be superlative across the board. While half the newly formed nations conformed to the definition of natural nations (two of them nearly so), even those that continued to be ethnically diverse showed outstanding social and economic progress since independence. Thus, independence appears to provide a fillip for social and economic progress even without ethnic homogeneity. This is rigorously shown to be the case for Montenegro, the only country with enough time series observations to do a structural break test.

The findings in this chapter should provide food for thought for global policy makers when considering the right of self-determination of citizens of natural nations, such as the Kashmiris, Kurds and Palestinians.

Notes

1 This comparison does not constitute an exact natural experiment since ethnic unity or diversity is not the only variable that comes into play in explaining economic and social performance.
2 Both Bangladesh and Pakistan are climate vulnerable. For Pakistan, this became very evident from the climate-exacerbated floods of summer 2022 (www.world-weatherattribution.org/climate-change-likely-increased-extreme-monsoon-rainfall-flooding-highly-vulnerable-communities-in-pakistan/, consulted September 17, 2022). Climate-induced change in rain patterns suggests both droughts and floods in the future, the latter exacerbated by glassier melts. The GERMANWATCH Global Climate Risk Index for 2021 ranked Bangladesh seventh and Pakistan eighth in terms of suffering most from extreme climate-related weather events between 2000 and 2019.
3 For the ethnic composition of Pakistan's army, refer to https://indianexpress.com/article/explained/pakistan-army-general-qamar-javed-bajwa-4412295/, consulted April 6, 2022.
4 Refer to Stewart (2000, Table 1) for a comprehensive documentation of possible dimensions across which ethnic or other group inequalities (referred to by her as horizontal inequalities) can exist.
5 "Over 200 nationalist activists in Sindh vow to quit separatism", *The Dawn*, March 24, 2022, www.dawn.com/news/amp/1681472, consulted February 24, 2022. Even so, insurgency in Sindh has not quite vanished, and it may be developing links with Balochi insurgency for joint operations, particularly against the Chinese. Refer to Mohammed Amir Rana, "Militancy in Sindh", *The Dawn International*, October 16, 2022, www.dawn.com/news/1715297, consulted December 5, 2022.
6 While foreign funding is very likely, it is up to the Pakistani leadership to ensure that the rights of provincial citizens are respected to avoid creating disruptive opportunities for those who seek to exploit them.
7 www.dawn.com/news/1734307, consulted April 19, 2023. The main administrative tiers under the province are divisions and districts.
8 For an anthropologist's account of the ethnic complexity of Pakistani society, refer to Ahmed (1987).
9 Khan (2022, Chapter 1, Appendix Tables 1.2b and f) estimated that Bangladesh's annual average per capita GDP growth between 2010 and 2018 was three times higher (5.4 percent compared to Pakistan's 1.8 percent).
10 Information available on the IMF website (www.imf.org/en/Home).
11 On November 9, the IMF announced that it had reached a staff-level agreement with Bangladesh under various facilities for a total package of $4.5 billion (www.imf.org/en/News/Articles/2022/11/08/pr22375-bangladesh, consulted April 19, 2023). COVID and the Russian-Ukraine War caused a drop in exports and a rise in oil, diesel and key commodity prices. The global economic crisis ushered in by the war is weighing heavily even on robust middle-income economies. Even so, unlike Sri Lanka and Pakistan, Bangladesh secured a stabilization rather than a bailout package, and Bangladesh's FOREX reserves when it sought IMF support had slipped from $39 billion to $32 billion (www.aljazeera.com/economy/2023/2/23/severe-dollar-crisis-hobbles-bangladesh-businesses). By contrast, Pakistan's FOREX reserves in April 2023 dipped to a precarious $3.1 billion as it awaited a decision on its IMF bailout package.
12 The lack of progress in Bangladesh over time is also evident from the average being very close to the terminal year, while for Pakistan the terminal year performance consistently dominates the average performance.
13 As indicated by Mondal (2000), prominent civil society organizations like BRAC (Originally Bangladesh Rural Advancement Committee and now Building

Resources Across Communities) and Proshika also played a prominent role as partners with the state in boosting Bangladesh's human development indicators.

14 As a percentage of GDP, Bangladesh's military expenditure started at 0.7 percent of GDP in 1972, peaked at 1.6 in 1999 and then steadily declined. The time series of Pakistan's military expenditure as a percentage of GDP is a little more difficult to summarize due to fluctuations. However, the broad story is that it started at 7 percent of GDP in 1972 and, with some fluctuations, hovered around 7 percent until 1992 and then steadily declined. However, as the numbers show, it remained about three times higher than Bangladesh in 2021 (data drawn from the World Bank, World Development Indicators, update March 30 2023, https://databank.worldbank.org/ reports.aspx?source=world-development-indicators#, consulted April 19, 2023).

15 However, there are limits to fellow feelings, even with ethnic homogeneity, in the private sector. The Rana Plaza disaster, whereby a factory burned down with workers locked inside without adequate exits, is a good example of this. Owners took short-cuts in terms of compliance with the code of conduct standards imposed by the buyers. Conditions are worse when multinational corporations, pressured by civil society where they are based, do not impose constraints via a code of conduct. Matters came to a head on April 24, 2013, due to the collapse of the Rana Plaza building in Dhaka, Bangladesh, which housed five ready-made garment (RMG) factories. The collapse resulted in the death of at least 1,132 people, and more than 2,500 workers were injured. This created a global uproar, and international garment brands provided assurance of lasting change. The International Labour Organization (ILO, https://www.ilo.org/infostories/en-GB/Stories/Country-Focus/rana-plaza, consulted February 2, 2021) reported that accidents continued apace despite the May 15, 2013, establishment of the Accord on Building and Fire Safety in Bangladesh, which was signed by the majority of western retailers and brands. A BBC podcast (*World Business Review*) on April 24, 2023, a decade after the disaster, reported that disabled families had still not been compensated, and BBC reported that relatives are still searching for missing victims (www.bbc.com/news/ av/world-asia-22522914, consulted April 25, 2023). On the positive side, Bangladesh Garments Manufacturer and Exporters Association (not an unbiased source) claimed to an Al Jazeera reporter that more than 80 percent of Bangladesh's 3,200 RMG factories are now internationally compliant with safety and security standards (www.aljazeera.com/news/2023/4/24/ten-years-of-rana-plaza-how-safe-is-bangladesh-garment-industry, consulted April 25, 2023). After the Accord expired in 2020, the RMG Sustainability Council (RSC), comprising RMG manufacturers, global brands and retailers and global unions and their Bangladeshi affiliates, took over the work. While constraints on capitalist ravages imposed by international and national civil society via pressure on the state can help, ultimately it will be the exhaustion of surplus labor (Lewis, 1954), as in China, which will secure a sustained better deal for workers.

16 In addition, North Macedonia, Montenegro and Serbia are candidates for accession and so have undertaken policies inducing more monetary and fiscal discipline.

17 The data for both series were drawn from the World Development Indicators (updated September 16, 2022), and the Chow test for structural breaks was conducted using EViews.

References

Ahmed, A.S. 1987. *Pakistan society: Islam, ethnicity and leadership in South Asia*. Karachi: Oxford University Press.

Gardezi, S.M.F., et al. 2015. 'National integration and cohesion in Pakistan: Voices from AJK', *Journal of Contemporary Studies*, 4(1), 57–80.

Khan, S.R. 2022. *Economic successes in South Asia: A story of partnerships*. New York: Routledge.

Khan, S.R. and Akhtar, A.S. with Bodla, S. 2014. *The military and development denied in the Pakistani Punjab: An eroding social consensus*. London: Anthem Press.

Lewis, W.A. 1954. 'Economic development with unlimited supplies of labor', *The Manchester School*, 22(2), 139–191.

Mondal, A.H. 2000. 'Social capital formation: The role of NGO rural development programs in Bangladesh', *Policy Sciences*, 33(3–4), 459–475.

Rodrik, D. 2015. 'Premature deindustrialization', *Journal of Economic Growth*, 21(1), 1–33.

Siddiqa, A. 2007. *Military Inc.: Inside Pakistan's military economy*. Karachi: Oxford University Press.

Stewart, F. 2000. 'Crisis prevention: Tackling horizontal inequalities', *Oxford Development Studies*, 28(3), 245–262.

5 Forging national cohesion in constructed nations

Introduction

Explicit or implicit in the findings of research is that the negative impact of ethnic fragmentation on economic growth and development could be offset with better institutions (Tan, 2010; La Porta et al., 1999). Chapter 1 makes the case that the starting point in highly ethnically fragmented nations (constructed nations) should be institution building to create national cohesion. This is supported by research documented in Chapter 3 demonstrating the positive impact of ethnic fragmentation on conflict and the negative impact of ethnic fragmentation on economic growth. Rodrik (1999) showed that ethnic cleavages mattered to the ability of governments to manage shocks and sustain economic growth, even when the quality of (New Institutional Economics [NIE] type) institutions as recommended by NIE is controlled for. Thus, the focus of this chapter is on identifying best practice for institution building that facilitates national cohesion.

The hypothesis explored in this book is that national cohesion, a prime trigger for catch-up growth, is more likely in natural nations with a common ethnicity. As defined in Chapter 2, ethnicity is used as a shorthand for a shared ethnic, linguistic, historic, cultural and religious identity. Nations without the national cohesion resulting from a common ethnicity, or from being a natural nation (90 percent plus common ethnicity), therefore need to find other paths to create national cohesion.[1]

This chapter first delineates some of the common strategies used for engendering national cohesion. Next it presents case studies of noted successes in creating national cohesion in multi-ethnic Tanzania and Ghana.[2] These strategies, if well utilized, can also undermine the attempt by political entrepreneurs to utilize ethnic fictionalization as a social cleavage for their own ambitions. Another case study documents Pakistan's struggle with handling ethnic separatism in Balochistan, one of its four provinces. This case study shows how Pakistan mishandled this ethnic conflict, providing political entrepreneurs with an opening, and some promising strategies being adopted for national reconciliation.

DOI: 10.4324/9781032630878-5

Strategies for building national cohesion

While the focus of much of the literature cited in Chapter 3 has been on the negative association of ethnic diversity on conflict and economic growth, Bornman (2019) cited studies by social psychologists indicating that ethnic loyalty has been found to play an important role in individual social and psychological well-being. Further, he found that ethnic group identification has more salience when individuals perceive their groups as being meted out unjust treatment.

Thus, nation building that celebrates rather than represses ethnic identity with inclusive and just policies and by removing group threats is a win-win. The two complementary country-wide strategies for attaining these objectives are federations and consociationalism, as discussed later.

Nation building has a long history and is not unique to nations constructed as an outcome of colonialism. For example, Alesina and Reich (2015) pointed out that in 1860, French was a foreign language for half of French children. Similarly, following the unification of Italy in 1860, only 10 percent of the population spoke what would become the Italian language. Both states pursued nation building policies to create the French and the Italians. These policies included a network of road and rail links traversing the country, state-controlled education with compulsory elementary education, aggressively enforced national language for schools, religious services and the administration and compulsory military service to mix and integrate individuals from different parts of the country.

Education is probably the most commonly used strategy for attaining national cohesion. Dryden-Peterson and Mulimbi (2017) explore how Botswana charted a pathway toward peace in spite of embodying the predictors of ethnic violence, that is, the existence of ethnic diversity (a dominant ethnic group and a plethora of smaller ones),[3] mineral wealth and low levels of education.

The leadership viewed education to be the most important instrument for nation building and ethnic peace. Botswana used its mineral wealth wisely for educational investment. It was wise not only because of the social returns to education but also because the investment was ethnically blind.[4] At the time of independence, only 20 percent of the population was enrolled in primary school, and it turned out only 100 secondary school graduates. It changed this scenario by being consistently among the highest investors in education as a percentage of gross domestic product (GDP) in the world (10 percent), and with its sizable mineral wealth, this was significant. About 50 years after independence, a child born in Botswana can, on average, expect 12.4 years of schooling, the highest in sub-Saharan Africa.

Initially, like France and Italy, Botswana's focus, embedded in the curriculum, was on creating national unity, and so the language and culture of the dominant ethnicity were privileged. This imposition on minority ethnicities created horizontal inequalities and unrest though not ethnic violence. Vision 2016 proposed educational reforms that recognized the importance of multi-culturalism and for a gradual transition to minority ethnicities being taught in their mother tongues from the language of the dominant ethnicity and English. The emphasis was on unity based on common heritage, goals and destiny rather than national unity simply based on an imposed common language and culture. This vision, however, has not been realized and remains a challenge for Botswana. However, the redistributive educational investment at a large scale may have promoted sufficient opportunity and national cohesion so that this challenge can be resolved peacefully.

The example of Botswana indicates that if ethnic diversity is perceived as a problem for social and economic progress, states are likely to search for mechanisms for promoting national cohesion. As mentioned in Chapter 2, there is much to learn from the democratic practice of current high-income countries (HICs). For example, Lephart (1977) discussed in detail the cases of Belgium, the Netherlands and Switzerland, which have a great deal of ethnic diversity – Belgium, in particular, has experienced ethnic tensions.

The democratic mechanism recommended by Lephart to mitigate such tensions is consociationalism or inclusive democracy, which includes the principles of a grand coalition, mutual veto (decision by consensus), proportionality in representation and autonomy. This amounts to recognizing and celebrating plurality rather than repressing it. Federalism that includes subnational autonomy via legislative devolution of political and fiscal authority is a logical approach when ethnicities are coeval with geographic boundaries. As will become evident when discussing the case studies of Tanzania, Ghana and Pakistan, these principles of consociationalism, adapted to local conditions, are embedded in current governance in these countries.

A review of the literature suggests other strategies, apart from those listed earlier, are utilized for nation building in constructed nations. Ahlerup et al. (2016) addressed the issue of what might enable a nation to sustain catch-up growth following a growth spurt (at least 2 percent growth lasting for at least five years). Using a dataset covering 20 sub-Saharan African countries from 1999 onward, their findings suggested that countries whose governments were perceived as impartial by the various ethnic groups residing in the country were more likely to experience sustained growth. By contrast, greater identification with the nation-state relative to ethnic groups did not matter for sustaining growth.

Blouin and Mukand (2019) evaluated the Rwandan government's efforts to reshape ethnic attitudes through radio propaganda. They did so by implementing a series of lab-in-the-field experiments that measured ethnic attitudes of 438 subjects in 52 villages in rural Rwanda. Their results showed that individuals exposed to Radio Rwanda placed lower salience on ethnicity, had higher inter-ethnic trust and were more willing to interact face-to-face with members of another ethnic group.[5]

Another policy for national cohesion in multi-ethnic societies is affirmative action. As mentioned in the preface, Pakistan adopted a quota system in 1948, one year after its independence, to give greater representation in politics, civil service and universities to the less developed regions. While East Pakistan was not given its due share, there are now greater shares for less developed regions than their share of the population.[6]

Sports can be another tool for dimming ethnic identities to forge a national one.[7] Using data from five waves of the Afro barometer survey with information on 69 official matches involving African teams between 2002 and 2015, covering over 37,000 respondents in 25 countries, Depetris-Chauvin et al. (2020) found evidence that national football (soccer) team success weakened ethnic identification, as opposed to national identity, improved attitudes toward other ethnicities and reduced inter-ethnic violence. The effect of victories corresponded to a 37 percent decrease in the average probability of ethnic self-identification and was quite persistent up to 30 days before and after the match. Post-victory respondents were also significantly more likely to trust and interact with members of other ethnicities.

For a second set of findings, they combined the football data with data on the occurrence and severity of political violence events, available from the Armed Conflict Location and Event Data Project (ACLED), for the period of 1997–2015. They found that countries whose teams (barely) qualified for the African Cup of Nations tournament experienced significantly less ethnic conflict in the following six months than countries whose teams (barely) did not. This effect was sizable and significant and lasted up to several months after the event. The effect of victories was stronger if the ethnic composition of the national team was more diverse.

The authors argue that even if the effects are transient, their results suggest that they may last long enough to open a precious window for political dialogue, negotiations and reforms capable of producing long-lasting improvements. However, there may be a limit to how far sports can go in creating national cohesion if ethnic or other fissures become very deep. For example, in Cameroon, Anglican separatists did not root for the national team to qualify for the 2022 World Cup in Football.[8]

Green (2019) found that ethnic homogenization (in terms of subjective identification) is associated with industrialization using various indicators of industrialization, such as carbon emissions, cement production, urbanization and agriculture's share in GDP. This amounts to saying that structural change associated with development may well automatically reduce ethnic tensions to some extent.

Social justice/inclusion is probably the most effective way of generating national cohesion. The Nordic social democracies created social cohesion based on high taxes and a solid safety net. Introduction of immigrants from different ethnicities is enlightened but inevitably results in social tension. In a survey on societal problems in Sweden, the highest loading (38 percent) was on integration and immigration. Integration takes at least a generation and sometimes more depending on social policies.[9] In this regard, nations more willingly open borders to others of similar ethnicity, as happened in Poland after Russia's invasion of Ukraine.[10]

Kpessa et al. (2011) argued that post-independence nationalist leaders in sub-Saharan Africa used social policy (health, housing and education programs) to foster a sense of national unity that would transcend the existing ethnic divisions created by the arbitrary drawing of state boundaries during colonization. These policies not only created national cohesion but also contributed to economic development by investing in social infrastructure and human capital.

The authors pointed out that this effort at creating national cohesion via social sector delivery was undermined by neo-liberal structural adjustment policies of the 1980s and 1990s that undermined social programs, notwithstanding World Bank's or the International Monetary Fund's (IMF) lip service to social delivery and social protection of the poor. Instead of the universal commitment to citizens, user fees were introduced. Privatization to increase efficiency enhanced unemployment and poverty. The paring back of the state created a vacuum that political entrepreneurs exploited, and ethnicity was fit for purpose. The authors noted that, in the same vein, neo-liberal Thatcher policies could be held responsible for the birth of Scottish nationalism.[11]

Resources to move to a social democratic model are not as readily available at least to low-income and low-middle-income countries (LICs/LMICs) without getting dangerously indebted. Sri Lanka and, more recently, Pakistan are cases in point. Sri Lanka has a long and commendable history of making social investments (Khan, 2022, Chapter 4). However, economic mismanagement, tax cuts, the loss of tourism and other export income after COVID along with those social commitments resulted in indebtedness reached a breaking point in the Spring of 2022. The currency collapsed, and this was accompanied by a shortage of key inputs and rampant inflation, which, in turn, triggered massive unrest.

Prime Minister of Pakistan Imran Khan (2018–2022), for all his political shortcomings, was consistently a sympathizer with the low-income citizens as demonstrated by his personal philanthropy prior to becoming prime minister. However, when in office, his pursuit of social democracy, such as by setting up an inclusive health care system and extending the social safety net, relied on heavy and unsustainable borrowing and debt levels. This resulted in a loss of confidence, a rapidly depreciating currency and high inflation. Of course, this is not a recommendation for withdrawing from social sector delivery but rather to more effectively mobilize domestic resources and target delivery.

One could argue that a natural corollary of the argument proffering national cohesion as a prime cause for catch-up growth is that countries that can successfully (or forcefully) integrate/assimilate their ethnolinguistic minorities would be more successful than those that have not or cannot. All political theorists would agree that force may temporarily provide the illusion of integration but that such cohesion is skin-deep and generates popular reactions.[12] In fact, all the case studies below militate against this logic of using force for integration or assimilation and suggest instead the use of inclusive policies to produce the right incentives for sustainable national cohesion.

Case studies[13]

Tanzania

Ndulu et al. (2019) pointed out that in contrast with Kenya, South Africa and Nigeria, Tanzania is a success story in creating a sense of nationhood despite containing 126 ethnic groups.[14] They give much of the credit to the founding father, Mwalimu Julius Kambarage Nyerere, who was determined to create this sense of nationhood and eliminate tribalism via abolishing chiefdoms, promoting Swahili as a national language, developing educational policies that promoted national unity and seeking to ensure equitable resource allocation within the country consistent with the Ashura Declaration.[15] Given Nyerere's reputation for high integrity, and consequently his popularity, he was able to attain much in this regard.

The education curriculum, with a focus on civics, sought to embed a shared national identity among the youth, and national consciousness was similarly promoted via adult literacy. Nyerere, himself a teacher, recognized the importance of education in creating national cohesion and inducing development. During the course of serving as president (1964–1985), literacy increased from a mere 15 percent of the population to about 60 percent (Muller, 2012).

Secondary schools were in short supply and thus required mobility and a mixing of ethnicities. This was further enhanced by compulsory national service instituted for all those completing secondary school and higher education programs. Notwithstanding the objections of those who had attained higher education in being temporarily relegated to a lower salary, this enabled young people to work together to build a sense of nationhood and develop cultural and sociological awareness of other ethnic groups. This also promoted inter-marriages between ethnic groups further forging a sense of nationhood. Finally, Nyerere initiated a policy of appointing officials to serve outside their home areas, and this continued after his departure from office. This policy was designed to mitigate nepotism while promoting inter-ethnic understanding.

The central government also took note of problems at the local level and sought to solve them at the national level rather than let ethnically based local associations develop to address them. For example, the central government took on the responsibility of funding new educational facilities and scholarships rather than leave this to ethnically based local cooperative societies.

When a particular locale ran out of farming land, the local party and government officials called on the central government to provide loans so that the young could start farming in other parts of the country or to work on state farms. The 2002 Political Parties Act instituted the principle that any political party must have support from across Tanzania's regions.

These policies met with considerable success. The authors cite the 2017 Afro barometer survey (Round 6) in which 97 percent of respondents said they had never been discriminated against because of their ethnicity, 98 percent had never suffered on account of their regional identity and 93 percent felt the government had never treated their ethnic group unfairly. Further, 96 percent of respondents either did not worry about or else liked having people from other ethnic groups as neighbors.

Using an earlier round (Round 4) of the Afro barometer survey, Muller (2012) noted that only 7 percent of the respondents identified themselves only in ethnic terms. Thus, it appears that national rather than ethnic identification in Tanzania has persisted despite Muller's concerns that economic problems might result in a reversal such that ethnic identification became predominant.

Langer et al. (2017) constructed a composite social cohesion index (SCI) based on responses on various rounds of the Afro barometer surveys (2005, 2008 and 2012). The three components of the index were based on elicited perceptions on inequality, trust and identity. Tanzania consistently ranked in the top three on the index, which ranged from 0 to 1 like the Human Development Index, although its score declined somewhat over time. The authors deflated the index, based on the variation in the SCI across ethnic groups, and Tanzania emerged with the highest rank in all three years (sharing the top position with Senegal in two of the three years).

This result was replicated by Bornman (2019), using the sixth round of the Afro barometer.

Ghana

Ghana presents another case study of a country that has successfully managed to diffuse political tensions based on ethnicity, thanks again in part to a charismatic founding leader (Kwame Nkrumah), who, according to McDonnell (2016), ensured regional public investment and public good provision (health, education, roads, electricity and industry) based on relative underdevelopment and not ethnicity. Nkrumah advocated posting teachers and boarding secondary school students outside of their home region, which, together with national universities, put young people into diverse groupings precisely at the time of dating and mate selection – hence, ensuring a high rate of inter-ethnic marriages (20 percent). Choosing English as the official state language meant no particular ethnic group was advantaged.[16]

McDonnell (2016) also pointed out that Ghana is among the 12 most ethnically diverse countries in the world.[17] Yet, it has had several peaceful power transitions through free and fair elections, avoided ethnic conflict and had no violent anti-government protest (one of six African countries in this regard). The Afro barometer showed it to rank high on social trust, satisfaction with health services and stated legitimacy of the tax system. While several of Nkrumah's policies failed, one enduring legacy has been the distribution of public goods based on factors such as pork barrel politics but not ethnicity.

Ghana's political success appears to result from a mix of consociationalism policies (see earlier) and a political communication strategy. Fosu (2021) argued that this relative success has been based on "purposive depoliticization of ethnicity". The 1956 election led to the passage of the Avoidance of Discrimination Act of 1957, which outlawed political parties based on ethnic, racial, regional or religious differences, and this act has featured in all subsequent constitutions. To win political power, a political party needs to mobilize across ethnic lines. This also means that political party leadership needs to cut across ethnic divides, so the choice of running mates with different ethnic backgrounds is part of a winning political strategy.[18]

Regional inclusion has been institutionalized in the constitution, which enjoins governing parties (presidents) to ensure regional representation in cabinet ministerial appointments. Ghana's political machinery rewards politicians who are "more adept at maneuvering the multi-social forces" than appealing to crude ethnic fissures. The latter is frowned upon and, to date, has been an election loser.[19]

Finally, in the interest of national peace and progress, politicians adopted the "peace-loving Ghanaian" trope as a communication strategy. Koter's (2021) research, based on purposive sample of 200 survey responses across the country, indicated how widely and deeply this sense of being "peace-loving" has become part of the national identity of Ghanaians.[20]

Langer (2009) addressed the puzzle of why, despite colonialism's exacerbation of large social and economic inequalities between the relatively prosperous south and the relatively impoverished and ethnically distinct north, ethnic conflict has not emerged. He attributed this non-conflict to several factors, including successive administrations that pursued politically, culturally and religiously inclusive policies. They also attempted to reduce the north-south development gap. Even if this was with limited success, the politically included northern elite was appeased.

Based on interviews, primary documents and foreign and local writings, Jonsson (2009) reported on inter-ethnic conflict between 1980 and 1995 in the northern region of Ghana that resulted in the death of thousands. While this represented a challenge to the image of Ghana as a peaceful country, the author conceded that since the Ghanaian political parties were mainly national, that prevented large-scale civil war along ethnic lines.[21] Further, the democratic system opened up political routes to ethnic prestige for northern elites. Also, economic improvements over time decreased the perceived desirability and viability of violent conflict. Finally, conflict in the northern region has been avoided via non-governmental organization (NGO) efforts to resolve conflicts peacefully. These are positive developments for containing future conflicts in the north even though the neutral state has not developed institutional mechanisms for conflict avoidance. Overall, Ghana has much to teach other countries, such as Pakistan, about containing ethnic violence.[22]

Pakistan

While Pakistan is not an acknowledged success story in dealing with ethnic discontent, its case is explored because it was severed into two because of ethnic conflict and is currently experiencing considerable ethnic disaffection. By trial and error, Pakistan has been moving to a model of governance that embodies several principles of consociationalism (see earlier). If these principles are well implemented, it might become an inclusive and viable democracy.

As indicated in Chapter 3, ethnic conflict in Pakistan has continued and has been one of the key factors in undermining political stability and economic progress. Balochistan constituted about half the land mass of the country though only about 5.5 percent of the population in 2022. It has experienced several waves of insurgency and presents Pakistani policy makers with a major challenge.

In 1947, when an independent Pakistan was created, Balochistan had the status of a princely state in which the Khan of Kalat was accepted by the other tribal *sardars* (chiefs) as the dominant *sardar*. The Khan had a treaty with the British allowing light touch governance. Access, as needed, such as to Afghanistan, was allowed the British in exchange for considerable autonomy.

It was made to accede to Pakistan in 1948 by the new Pakistani state, with British approval, against the Khan of Kalat's will. This was the original source of Balochi resentment and insurgency. Subsequently, there have been four waves of insurgencies (Alamgir, 2012; Wani, 2021b)[23] due to the federal government's high-handedness and the view that its resources have been usurped by the elites of other provinces, mostly the Punjab, much as East Pakistan claimed was the case before its successful liberation struggle in 1971.[24]

There is truth to Balochistan's claims. It is the richest province in terms of natural resources but the poorest in terms of social and economic development (Bengali, 2018). It is underrepresented in all federal institutions including the courts, military[25] and bureaucracy. Even within Balochistan, Balochis are notably underrepresented in development projects initiated by the federal government (Wani, 2021b).

Natural gas was discovered in Sui, Balochistan, in 1952 and started being piped mainly to Punjab and Sindh in 1955. Gas connections did not become available in the provincial capital Quetta until 1970, by some accounts, and that too initially to provide connections to an army cantonment (Wani, 2021b). A shortage of natural gas supply in the province was more recently reflected by a statement of the Balochistan minister for petroleum and natural resources, Mr. Jam Kamaal, who in 2015 said, "We are considering the option of importing Sui gas from Iran."[26] In fact, in violation of the constitution, Sui, a mere four miles from the site of the gas discovery, has no gas connections since elites do not reside there.[27] It is not surprising then that separatists target gas pipelines.

The political and military elites governing Pakistan and its provinces are determined not to let history repeat itself, in the form of a successful liberation struggle, via repression, and thus have fanned a vicious cycle of violence and counterviolence.[28] A much more sensible approach would be inclusion via a fair distribution of resources. Inclusion here means not only that the income-poor provinces get a fair share of their own resources but also that low-income citizens in the income-poor provinces are similarly included.[29]

Major development projects are underway or planned in Balochistan, and this presents the federal government an opportunity to ensure inclusion, as defined earlier, and diffuse Balochi resource nationalism. A good start has been made with regard to the copper and gold mines in Reko Diq.[30] These mines are considered to be among the largest in the world and are expected to yield about $100 billion over their lifetime and generate $1 billion a year in annual revenues. After a mis-start, the final agreement between the foreign investor and the federal and provincial governments is expected to yield an investment of $10 billion in Balochistan.[31] It includes the creation of 8,000 local jobs, $1 billion spent in social uplift projects and 25 percent of profits, in addition to royalties and other financial benefits for the provincial exchequer (without any investment/expense), with the rest going to foreign and local investors.[32] Both the provincial and federal governments need to monitor that income-poor Balochis actually benefit from the agreement.[33]

This agreement could be a template for resolving another flashpoint that has resulted in Balochi protests. Gwadar port, planned for construction in 1992, was initiated with Chinese assistance in 2002. It was subsequently included as a key part of China's Belt and Road Initiative, locally termed the China-Pakistan Economic Corridor (CPEC), in 2015. It was initially welcomed by locals, but the typical high-handedness of the federal government in claiming jurisdiction over the port and giving locals no say in the decision making or in operation and maintenance sparked the ire of separatists.

Rafiq (2021) provided an account of why the Pakistan state's hope for the port becoming another Singapore was misplaced and why trickle down has been slow to materialize. Ahmad (2017) indicated how locals in Gwadar continue to be deprived of social and physical infrastructure. Land grabbing by the federal government and non-locals at bargain basement prices added to the resentment (Wani, 2021b).

Another grievance is the access of local fisherfolk to their traditional fishing sites, which are blocked by newly constructed highways or by security considerations. More aggravation results from fishing grounds raided by non-locals, including Chinese trawlers, and these grievances have sparked protests. Rafiq (2021) sees promise for the project in the intermediate and long term but suggests that all planning should include locals and that project benefits to them, in terms of scarce water, power, health and education, should be front-loaded going forward to win local confidence.

Political scientists and international relations scholars have written on Balochi insurgencies, with the articles published in Indian journals (Wani, 2021a, 2021b), assuming different positions from those in Pakistani (Ahmad, 2017) or international journals (Alamgir, 2012; Siddiqi, 2012; Mushtaq and Mirza, 2022). However, there is consensus that inclusive policies are called for to ameliorate Balochi resentments.[34] These resentments have, at times, caused a virtual boycott of electoral politics.[35]

The suggestion about inclusiveness also applies to the other non-dominant ethnicities in other provinces. For a constructed nation like Pakistan, comprising many different ethnicities (see Chapter 4), national cohesion paradoxically needs to be based on letting ethnicities flourish. Kanbur et al. (2011, p. 152) pointed out that India's linguistic reorganization of polity in the 1950s and 1960s was widely viewed as a great institutional success. By giving each major language group a stake in the India federation, Indian decision makers removed a great source of ethnic grievance from politics such as the one that initiated the tension between East and West Pakistan when the latter tried to impose Urdu as the lingua franca. A long democratic tradition since independence promoted both inclusion and relative political stability.[36]

Some positive steps have been taken by elected governments in Pakistan, unlike the military governments that have had centralizing instincts.[37] Progress on provincial autonomy resulted from the Eighteenth Amendment to the Constitution.[38] The Seventh National Finance Commission Award for the distribution of provincial resources recognized the need for national cohesion via distribution based on considerations other than population such as inverse population density and poverty, both of which benefit the less well-off provinces and Balochistan in particular.

Making provinces more fully coterminous with ethnicity may also help.[39] For example, allowing Saraikistan and Hazara to become separate provinces and allowing Pushtun areas in North Balochistan to merge with Khyber-Pakhtunkhwa, if there is a demand for it by both ethnicities, would help.[40] Not counting the diaspora, there are a significant number of Baloch in bordering states including Iran (up to two million) and Afghanistan (up to two million). Ideally, all Baloch should reside in a natural nation, but that does not seem politically feasible. However, provincial autonomy and a fair share of their natural resources are politically feasible and may end insurgency.[41]

There is hope that strengthened institutions in Pakistan like the National Finance Commission and the courts, after about 75 years of independence at the time of writing, will act to promote justice for the more income-poor provinces in federal-provincial and inter-provincial relations to enhance national consensus. On April 8, 2022, the Islamabad High Court directed the president of Pakistan to hear the grievances of Balochi students of Quaid-e-Azam University, Pakistan's premier public university, in particular of their fear of being abducted if they returned to their home province.[42]

An increasingly independent judiciary and Election Commission are enhancing confidence by challenging political authorities at the highest level.[43] Other institutions designed to promote national cohesion are also maturing and strengthening. A constitutionally founded Council of Common Interests (CCI) is a high-level body in the country for engendering inter-provincial harmony.[44]

Pakistan is a water-scarce country, and this has created disharmony between Punjab and Sindh in terms of water sharing. On March 31, 2022, in a technical committee meeting of the Indus River System Authority (IRSA), a major step forward was taken in this decade-old dispute. Both provinces agreed to open up their waterways to mutual inspection and to allow surprise visits to verify each other's data.[45]

Another body for promoting inter-provincial harmony is the National Economic Council. It is constituted by the president but chaired by the prime minister. It includes the chief ministers of all the provinces and a member nominated by them. Its purview is a discussion of economic issues of national concern and of concern to the provinces.

Summing up, Pakistan has made much progress in moving to national cohesion by utilizing the principles of consociationalism and federalism.

However, it does have a long way to go. Of late (Spring 2023), even the Supreme Court seemed to be getting politicized in the fractionalized and dysfunctional political struggles in Pakistan, and political commentators suggest it is in need of judicial reform. However, it is through such struggles that political maturity evolves, and even after almost 250 years, US democracy is still not free from such challenges. However, its major success has been to keep the military firmly in the barracks, as did India from the get-go, and this key democratic achievement has as yet eluded Pakistani democracy. This needs to be a key objective to strengthen democracy and attain national cohesion.[46]

Conclusion

Several strategies are proposed in the literature that can help enhance national cohesion in constructed nations. In terms of broad political strategies, consociationalism policies and federations can contain ethnic tensions. When ethnicities are coeval with geographies, federations are a preferable choice that can be complemented with consociationalism policies. Founding leaders with broad national visions such as Nyerere and Nkrumah have left enduring legacies of inter-ethnic harmony by making public policy ethnically blind.

Even if solid foundations of ethnic harmony have not been established, policies can mitigate tensions. Social policies, affirmative action and redistributive policies have been used in this regard and, if perceived to be fair, can certainly help. Sports can cement national cohesion, but it cannot help with festering resentments that need to be addressed first. Social democratic policies can address ethnic inequalities, but most L/LMICs lack the resources for them. The steps taken to ameliorate ethnic Balochi resentment and conflict in Pakistan represent a possible path for policy.

This ethnic tension and conflict in Pakistan suggest that three mechanisms are especially important for creating national cohesion in constructed nations. First, the perception among the diverse ethnicities that the federation is being just in allowing them full participation in the management and fair share of resources found within their geographies. Second, that the formula used by the federal authority in allocating federally mobilized resources is just. Finally, that the institutions designed to create inter-provincial or ethnic harmony are allowed to mature and strengthen to build national cohesion.

While Pakistan's ethnic tensions have not been fully resolved, political institutions, legislated and enacted by political governments, such as the CCI, National Finance Commission and National Economic Council and Devolution, seem to have gone some way to resolving them. It is interesting that the institutions designed to enhance national cohesion are overtly political in nature rather than simply pro-business.[47]

Pakistan's case is an interesting one in terms of the interface of ethnicity and religion. If religion always trumped ethnicity, Pakistan should not have had to struggle with creating national cohesion since all ethnicities are Muslims. The fact that politicians and scholars alike have highlighted that ethnic discord has undermined its social and economic progress suggests that religion alone cannot induce national cohesion.[48] Religion and ethnicity interact in complex ways, and what prevails as dominant at a particular historical juncture depends on circumstances including politics and the role of political entrepreneurs. This is evident, for example, in current-day India, which is constitutionally[49] secular and has had a history from its foundation as being avowedly secular. Even so, a political entrepreneur and opportunist like Narendra Singh Modi has undermined that history in a very short period of time by exploiting a religious social cleavage.

The case studies of Ghana and Tanzania suggest that while policies instituted by various constructed nations can be helpful for the needed institution building, each constructed nation will need to find its own mechanisms. Good leadership can certainly help in this regard. The important commonality is that national cohesion can only be born from inclusive policies and not force. Such inclusive policies are also the best antidote against political opportunists seeking power by exploiting ethnic cleavages.

In an ideal world, the best option is for ethnicities to be granted the right of self-determination based on plebiscites. For example, the logical conclusion based on the thesis propounded in this book about natural nations is that the ethnic Russian majorities in Crimea and parts of the Donbas region be granted a plebiscite under UN auspices to either stay with Ukraine or join Russia. This would be a preferred outcome to the armed conflict instigated by Russia.

Similarly, another logical conclusion is that the right of self-determination be granted to ethnicities struggling to become natural nations. However, history repeatedly shows that dominant ethnicities view separatism as weakening the federating unit, particularly if it means a loss of resources. Biafra, Tamil Nadu, Kurdistan, Mindanao and Kashmir[50] are examples of nations, based on ethnicity and/or religion, that have not been born yet due to violent repression by the dominant ethnicities or states. However, since the world is not ideal, the second-best option is for constructed nations to pursue strategies rooted in inclusion and social justice.

Notes

1 Other terms used in the literature for national cohesion include "national integration", "national harmony", "national solidarity", "national identity" and "social cohesion".
2 Malawi and Zambia, as mentioned in Chapter 2, are also notable for relative ethnic harmony and call for deeper exploration. Zambia's case has a similarity with Ghana and Tanzania, in that a charismatic founding leader (Kenneth Kawanda) emphasized unity and nation building.

3 Twenty-one at the last count.

4 The authors point to examples such as Nepal and pre-genocide Rwanda in which educational investment favored particular ethnic groups.

5 Film can also contribute to uniting nations. Refer to https://www.economist.com/asia/2023/09/14/how-to-unite-india-bollywood-style, consulted 10/4/2023.

6 Abdul Wajid Rana, "Quota system in Pakistan", *The Express Tribune*, November 09, 2017, https://tribune.com.pk/story/1553353/6-quota-system-pakistan, consulted May 25, 2022.

7 Refer to Darby (2013) on Nkrumah's employment of football to promote national unity and patriotic consciousness in Ghana – in addition to pan-African solidarity. Darby pointed out that, while to some extent politicizing football backfired for Nkrumah, since then, virtually, every Ghanaian head of state has recognized the "political utility" of football.

8 www.bbc.com/news/world-africa-60861896, consulted March 25, 2022.

9 www.statista.com/statistics/653876/survey-on-important-societal-issues-in-sweden/, consulted April 4, 2022.

10 While this resulted in charges of racism in the media, suspicion and mistreatment of the "other" seem a near-universal phenomenon.

11 A dissenting view is that that Scotland is massively subsidized by England even after accounting for potential tax revenue/royalties from North Sea oil but that ethnic entrepreneurs of the Scottish National Party have successfully created a sense of ethnic grievance and exploitation among a substantial portion of the Scottish populace. Others contend that there is no taxpayer subsidy from England to Scotland (www.thenational.scot/politics/19921421.english-taxpayers-subsidise-scotland-really-works/, consulted December 5, 2022).

12 The examples of protests in Iran against forcibly inducing a particular interpretation of Islam and in China against the heavy-handed COVID policy demonstrated this point. Other examples include protests against pension reform in France and judicial reform in Israel (Spring 2023). History is rife with examples of protest against forcible and high-handed state policy.

13 Sriskandarajah (2005) documents how inclusive policies in Malaysia, Mauritius and Trinidad and Tobago kept feared ethnic conflict at bay. The author argued that forging a partnership between the major constituent ethnic groups for negotiated economic redistribution was a central feature of the strategy for attaining inter-ethnic harmony. For example, in Malaysia, the grand bargain was "equal political rights to non-Malays within a secular country in return for the recognition of the special status of Malays, alongside indigenous people of the eastern states, as the Bumiputera ('sons of the soil')". This represents an example of "consociational democracy". Aided by measures embodied in the New Economic Policy and other initiatives, the gap between Malays and other ethnic groups closed in numerous areas of the economy. While inclusive policies kept ethnic conflict at bay, the author warned that a country cannot rest on its laurels and needs to be vigilant and active in updating policy, based on evidence, to ensure ethnic harmony.

14 Miller (2012) noted that since the largest ethnic group accounted for 13 percent of the population, with several others close by in population size, this helped in avoiding dominance and conflict. Pre-colonial inter-ethnic group relations were mostly congenial, and this also helped in creating a sense of national identity and cohesion.

15 As Miller (2012) and other scholars pointed out, Nyerere also supported one-party rule to create national cohesion and for the same reasons supported egalitarian policies such as the community-oriented *ujamaa* village initiative. While these policies did not survive his term in office, the consensus is that they probably helped in creating national cohesion. Nyerere himself realized toward the end of his term in office the necessity of political competition.

16 However, Kaplan (2009) noted that all major indigenous languages were utilized for teaching and in television and radio.

17 Also refer to Langer (2009) for details.

18 Ethnic power-sharing also intersects with religion (mainly a Christian-Islamic alliance).

19 Notwithstanding the accolades Ghana has garnered in the literature as a model of inter-ethnic harmony, Atuire (2020) sounded a word of caution regarding the infusion of ethnicity into politics. Thus, nations need to stay ever vigilant to prevent politicians being tempted to exploit ethnicity. In Ghana's case, since this practice is against the constitution, enforcement of the law could check it.

20 Of course, ethnic harmony does not imply a complete absence of protest. Al-Jazeera, on June 1, 2022, reported,

> [H]undreds took to the streets in Ghana's capital Accra for two days in late June to protest against spiraling inflation and other woes. Growth slowed to 3.3 percent year-on-year in the first quarter of 2022 and inflation hit a record of 27.6 percent in May.

The fall out of COVID and the Russian-Ukraine War spared few L/LMICs.

21 It bears mentioning that the local financing of the Volta River Project (one strongly pushed by Nkrumah) entailed raising taxes on cocoa farmers, and this led to some inter-provincial/ethnic resentment.

22 Langer et al. (2009) point out that Nigeria, which has the same kind of north-south divide, confronted much more ethnic conflict and the steps it has taken, with some success, to diffuse the ethnic tension.

23 Wani (2021b) pointed out that the current fifth wave is different in that it is pan-tribal and spearheaded by a young middle-class leadership, rather than tribal *sardars*, seeking separation rather than more provincial autonomy.

24 Apart from insurgency, the political dynamics in the first two decades of the twenty-first century in Balochistan have become highly complex. There has been the rise of Islamic jihadi militancy (supporting the Afghan Taliban via the Quetta Shura), the Tehrik-e-Taliban Pakistan (TTP, formed 2007) and sectarian violence by Punjab-based Sunni Lashkar-e-Jhangvi on Balochi Hazara Shia. Further, there is the militancy of the Sunni Balochi organization (Jundullah) across the border in Shia-majority Iran using Pakistani Balochistan as a base and ostensibly supported by the United States to undermine Iran. Iran has returned the favor by providing a base to Pakistani-based separatist organizations, as has Afghanistan. The US-China rivalry (dubbed the New Great Game) also plays out in Balochistan, both because of its strategic location and, for China, the lure of a warm water port vital for the development of Western China and its rich natural resource base (Siddiqi, 2012; Wani, 2021b).

25 Fair and Nawaz (2011) documented that in an effort to attract more officers from Sindh and Balochistan, the Pakistan Army relaxed the academic and testing requirements for recruitment in the early 1990s. Balochi and Sindhi recruits were favored in two ways: first, their threshold scores for passing were lower than for others (minimum score of 45 percent instead of 50 percent on intelligence tests), and second, they did not have to be placed as highly on the merit list due to a quasi-quota system in effect for selection. Data made available by the military from 1974 to 2005 to one of the authors demonstrated, with caveats, that the Pakistan Army has been successful in making the army more geographically representative with regard to the officer core recruiting, although some Balochi districts still showed an absence of recruiting. Even so, compared to 1974, officers in 2005 were being recruited from virtually all districts in the country. By 2005, Punjab's share of officer recruits was roughly proportional to its population share as was the case for Balochistan. Much progress was made in recruiting in Sindh, though it remained underrepresented while Khyber-Pakhtunkhwa was overrepresented.

26 In Pakistan, natural gas is referred to as Sui gas given its origin in Sui, Balochistan.
27 https://globalvoices.org/2015/05/20/why-is-pakistans-balochistan-shut-out-of-its-own-natural-gas-reserves/, consulted April 1, 2022.
28 While repression, including abduction and disappearances, might be more success-ful in a contiguous territory, unlike in East Pakistan, this does not mean it is the right thing to do. People have serious grievances that have not been addressed if they are willing to take up arms.
29 Refer to Mushtaq and Mirza (2022) for an account of how the tribal *sardars* com-plicate social investments in and transfers to the income-poor Balochis. Militancy against the federal state may have given the *sardari* system a lease on life since the focus is the exploitation by the outsider. The exploitation of the *sardars* is more likely to come into focus if the federal government manages to appease the militants with inclusive policies, especially since some of the militant groups espouse radical social philosophy.
30 The agreement is an improvement over the contentious wrangling between the fed-eral and the provincial governments of Balochistan over the Saindak Copper-Gold project initiated in 1995 (Wani, 2021a; https://en.wikipedia.org/wiki/Saindak_Cop-per_Gold_Project, consulted April 13, 2022).
31 On December 10, 2022, the Supreme Court endorsed the deal. Sohail Khan, "Supreme Court endorses landmark Reko Diq deal", *The Express Tribune*, Decem-ber 10, 2022, www.thenews.com.pk/print/1018492-sc-endorses-landmark-reko-diq-deal, consulted December 10, 2022. On December 16, 2022, the federal government and the government of Balochistan signed the deal with Barrick Gold. Saleem Sha-hid, "Govt, Barrick Gold sign final accord on Reko Diq", *The Dawn*, December 16, 2022, www.dawn.com/news/1726572, consulted December 16, 2022.
32 Syed Irfan Raza, "Pakistan signs deal to avoid $11bn penalty in Reko Diq case", *The Dawn*, March 22, 2022, www.dawn.com/news/1681071, and "Saudi firm to help Pakistan assess Reko Diq gold, copper quantity", *The Dawn*, March 27, 2022, www.dawn.com/news/1682029/saudi-firm-to-help-pakistan-assess-reko-diq-gold-copper-quantity, consulted April 5, 2022; Hasnaat Maik, "Pakistan evades $11b Reko Diq penalty", *The Express Tribune*, March 20, 2022, https://tribune.com.pk/story/2348850/pakistan-evades-11b-reko-diq-penalty, consulted April 8, 2022.
33 As suggested earlier, it is often alleged that, over the years, federal attempts to help low-income Balochis via various distributional schemes have been ineffective because of resource capture by tribal *sardars*. *Sardars* are generally viewed to be held in high regard by tribal members with a patronage system cementing this loyalty.
34 McMurry (2022) found empirical support from the Philippines for the view that recognition of traditional community rights led to greater engagement with formal state institutions, using birth registration as a measure. Her exploratory analyses from a survey experiment also supported the view that rights recognition could encourage greater affinity with the broader nation and more positive attitudes toward the state. Finally, she cited other studies supportive of this finding and against the conventional view that nation building is a zero-sum game and that subnational autonomy comes at the expense of nation building.
35 In 2013, Abdul Qudoos Bizenjo, the current chief minister of the province (2022), was elected to the Balochistan Assembly with only 544 votes, less than 1 percent of total registered voters in his constituency (https://tribune.com.pk/story/2357372/balochistan-politics, consulted May 20, 2022).
36 India Gandhi's emergency and the current administration's high-handedness will be, in the broad sweep of history, viewed as black marks (one ongoing) on an oth-erwise enviable political record.
37 Zulfiqar Ali Bhutto, an elected prime minister, and General Zia-ul-Haq, a mili-tary dictator, were notable exceptions to this trend in their treatment of Balochistan (Wani, 2021a).

38 http://cppg.fccollege.edu.pk/18th-amendment-implications-for-provincial-autonomy-and-governance/, consulted April 6, 2022.

39 Inter-mixing of ethnicities with the onset of national cohesion is inevitable over time. However, population movements for livelihood prior to such cohesion can be problematic. Apart from Balochi tribes, Balochistan contains sizable populations of Brahuis, Hazaras, Punjabis, Pashtuns, Sindhis and Saraikis. As indicated in the text, large development projects in Balochistan generate an influx of immigrants making Balochis fearful of becoming a minority in their province. Of the 12 million now living in Balochistan, 5.2 million are non-Balochi. This fear instigated a spate of killings by separatists of non-Balochis, mostly Punjabis and also Chinese, working and living in Balochistan as skilled and unskilled workers and professionals. The result was a massive move back, of about 100,000 settlers, to their home province (Siddiqi, 2012) and of heightened security for the Chinese. It bears mentioning that not only individual Balochis but also historically whole Baloch tribes have settled and assimilated in the other provinces of Pakistan, particularly in adjoining Sindh, in search of livelihoods (https://en.wikipedia.org/wiki/Baloch_diaspora, consulted April 8, 2022).

40 Interestingly, the Baloch nationalists are willing to concede Baloch territory in North Balochistan to Pashtuns and retain a more ethnically pure Balochistan (Siddiqi, 2012).

41 https://en.wikipedia.org/wiki/Baloch_people, consulted April 7, 2022.

42 Saqib Bashir, "IHC directs President Alvi to meet Baloch students", *The Express Tribune*, April 8, 2022, https://tribune.com.pk/story/2351511/ihc-directs-president-alvi-to-meet-baloch-students, consulted April 8, 2022.

43 On April 7, 2022, the Supreme Court refused to accept Prime Minister Imran Khan's attempt to avoid a vote of no confidence in Parliament by calling for snap elections after instructing the president to dissolve the assemblies. The legal argument used was the "doctrine of necessity", one the military has used in Pakistan to suspend the assemblies and assume power. The apex court has therefore also implicitly put the military on notice in terms of direct rule. The military however continues to wield political power indirectly.

44 The CCI's members are the prime minister (who cannot delegate his role to a minister), the chief ministers of the four provinces and three representatives of the federal government nominated by the prime minister. CCI meetings are to occur at least once every 90 days and are to be chaired by the prime minister. Decisions are taken by simple majority. The CCI is to have a permanent secretariat with representation from all the provinces and regions based on quotas.

45 Ahmad Faraz Khan, "Sindh, Punjab move closer to resolving water issues", *The Dawn*, April 7, 2022, www.dawn.com/news/1683830, consulted April 10, 2022.

46 The military's huge claim on national resources, as indicated in Chapter 4; hindrance of peace with India initiated by politicians so that relations can be normalized; and interference in the political process all impede national cohesion. In this regard, refer to Foqia Khan, "Did the establishment collude with Modi on Kashmir?" *The Friday Times*, April 30, 2023, www.thefridaytimes.com/2023/04/30/did-the-establishment-collude-with-modi-on-kashmir/, consulted April 30, 2023.

47 See, for example, the emphasis on pro-business institutions mentioned by Easterly (2001).

48 The discord is, of course, magnified by sectarian differences in religion.

49 The Forty-Second Amendment to the Indian Constitution, enacted in 1976, and the Preamble to the Constitution assert that India is a secular nation.

50 All these separatist movements have complicated histories, and the interested reader can easily find the relevant documentation to multifaceted perspectives.

References

Ahlerup, P., Baskaran, T. and Bigsten, A. 2016. 'Government impartiality and sustained growth in sub-Saharan Africa', *World Development*, 83(C), 54–69.

Ahmad, M. 2017. 'New great game and the CPEC in Balochistan: Opportunities and challenges', *Pakistan Journal of History and Culture*, 38(1), 83–108.

Alamgir, A. 2012. 'Pakistan's Balochistan problem: An insurgency's rebirth', *World Affairs*, 175(4), 33–38.

Alesina, A. and Reich, B. 2015. 'Nation Building', NBER Working Paper 18839, Boston, MA.

Atuire, C. A. 2020. 'Pursuing nation building within multi-partisan fragmentation: The case of Ghana', *National Identities*, 22(5), 533–547.

Bengali, K. 2018. *A cry for justice: Empirical insights from Balochistan*. Karachi: Oxford University Press.

Blouin, A. and Mukand, S.W. 2019. 'Erasing ethnicity? Propaganda, nation building, and identity in Rwanda', *Journal of Political Economy*, 127(3), 1008–1062.

Bornman, E. 2019. 'National versus ethnic identification in countries of the Southern African Development Community (SADC)', *Journal of Psychology in Africa*, 29(1), 22–29.

Darby, P. 2013. 'Let us rally around the flag: Football, nation building, and Pan-Africanism in Kwame Nkruma's Ghana', *The Journal of African History*, 54(2), 221–246.

Depetris-Chauvin, E., Durante, R. and Campante, F. 2020. 'Building nations through shared experiences: Evidence from African Football', *American Economic Review*, 110(5), 1572–1602.

Dryden-Peterson, S. and Mulimbi, B. 2017. 'Pathways toward peace: Negotiating national unity and ethnic diversity through education in Botswana', *Comparative Education Review*, 61(1), 58–82.

Easterly, W. 2001. 'Can institutions resolve ethnic conflict?', *Economic Development and Cultural Change*, 49(4), 687–706.

Fair, C.C. and Nawaz, S. 2011. 'The changing Pakistan Army Officer Corp', *The Journal of Strategic Studies*, 34(1), 63–94.

Fosu, R. 2021. 'When an African country avoids conflict: Purposive actions and actors in post-colonial state-building in Ghana', *South African Journal of International Affairs*, 28(1), 93–113.

Green, E. 2019. 'Industrialization and ethnic change in the modern world', *Ethnic and Racial Studies*, 42(2), 178–197.

Jonsson, J. 2009. 'The overwhelming minority: Inter-ethnic conflict in Ghana's northern region', *Journal of International Development*, 21(4), 507–519.

Kanbur, R., Rajaram, P.K. and Varshney, A. 2011. 'Ethnic diversity and ethnic strife. An interdisciplinary perspective', *World Development*, 39(2), 147–158.

Kaplan, S. 2009. 'Identity in fragile states: Social cohesion and state building', *Development*, 52(4), 466–472.

Khan, S.R. 2022. *Economic successes in South Asia: A story of partnerships*. New York: Routledge.

Koter, D. 2021. 'Accidental nation-building in Africa', *Nations and Nationalism*, 27(3), 862–879.

Kpessa, M., Béland, D. and Lecours, A. 2011. 'Nationalism, development, and social policy: The politics of nation-building in sub-Saharan Africa', *Ethnic and Racial Studies*, 34(12), 2115–2133.

Langer, A. 2009. 'Living with diversity: The peaceful management of horizontal ine-qualities in Ghana', *Journal of International Development*, 21(4), 534–546.

Langer, A., Mustapha, A.R. and Stewart, F. 2009. 'Diversity and discord: Ethnicity, horizontal inequalities and conflict in Ghana and Nigeria', *Journal of International Development*, 21(4), 477–482.

Langer, A., Stewart, F., Smedts, K. and Demarest, L. 2017. 'Conceptualizing and meas-uring social cohesion in Africa: Towards a perceptions-based index', *Social Indicators Research*, 131, 321–343.

La Porta, R., Lopez-de-Silanes, F., Shleifer, A. and Vishny, R. 1999. 'The quality of government', *The Journal of Law, Government, Economics and Organization*, 15(1), 222–279.

Lephart, A. 1977. *Democracy in plural societies: A comparative exploration*. New Haven, CT: Yale University Press.

McDonnell, E.M. 2016. 'Elite ethno-demographics and the puzzle of public goods within diverse African states', *Comparative Political Studies*, 49(11), 1513–1549.

McMurry, N. 2022. 'From recognition to integration: Indigenous autonomy, state authority, and national identity in the Philippines', *American Political Science Review*, 116(2), 547–563.

Muller, B. 2012. 'A success story of creating national identity in Tanzania: The vision of Julius Kambarage Nyerere', in Höllinger, F. and Hadler, M. (eds.) *Crossing borders, shifting boundaries*. Chicago, IL: University of Chicago Press, 125–148.

Mushtaq, M. and Mirza, Z.S. 2022. 'Understanding the nexus between horizontal ine-qualities, ethno-political conflict and political participation: A case study of Balo-chistan', *Ethnopolitics*, 21(3), 221–237.

Ndulu, B.J., Mbowe, W.E. and Hunter, E. 2019. 'Ethnicity, citizenry, and nation-building in Tanzania', in Hino, H., Langer, A., Lonsdale, J. and Stewart, F. (eds.) *From divided pasts to cohesive futures: Reflections on Africa*. New York: Cambridge University Press, 98–122.

Rafiq, A. 2021. 'Pakistan wanted Gwadar to be the next Singapore. China's role did not help. Protest at port city should be wake-up call for Islamabad', *Foreign Policy*, https://foreignpolicy.com/2021/12/14/pakistan-gwadar-port-protests-china-belt-and-road-cpec/?gclid=EAIaIQobChMI_v220Pj89gIVD43ICh2XdQz6EAAYAiAAEg-KYhPD_BwE, consulted 4/5/2022.

Rodrik, D. 1999. 'Where did all the growth go? External shocks, social conflict, and growth collapses', *Journal of Economic Growth*, 4(4), 385–412.

Siddiqi, F.H. 2012. 'Security dynamics in Pakistani Balochistan: Religious activism and ethnic conflict in the war on terror', *Asian Affairs: An American Review*, 39(3), 157–175.

Sriskandarajah, D. 2005. 'Development, inequality and ethnic accommodation: Clues from Malaysia, Mauritius and Trinidad and Tobago', *Oxford Development Studies*, 33(1), 63–79.

Tan, C.M. 2010. 'No true path: Uncovering the interplay between geography, insti-tutions, and fractionalization in economic development', *Journal of Applied Econo-metrics*, 25(7), 1100–1127.

Wani, S.A. 2021a. 'The Baloch insurgency in Pakistan and the Chinese connection', *Kulturni Studia*, 17(2), 82–99.

Wani, S.A. 2021b. 'The new Baloch Militancy: Drivers and dynamics', *India Quar-terly*, 77(3), 479–500.

6 Summary and conclusion

The contributions of New Institutional Economics (NIE) to development economics are formidable and have been incorporated into the World Bank and the International Monetary Fund's (IMF's) neo-liberal approach to reforming low- and low-middle-income countries (L/LMICs) that seek their assistance. In this regard, they have reshaped international development thinking and policy. While acknowledging the importance of these contributions, this book argues that there are a couple of critical gaps in NIE contributions to development economics.

Chapter 1 discusses the works of Douglas North and Daron Acemoglu and James A. Robinson as prominent contributions to thinking in development economics as part of the NIE approach. While there are important differences in detail, these authors emphasize the importance of inclusive institutions to facilitate economic freedoms and thereby social and economic development. Inclusive institutions are important because they harness the productive potential of the bulk of a nation's population.

The important question then is how these institutions evolve. The reference here is to institutions that deliver the rule of law, property rights and contract enforcement, which, in turn, constrain predatory behavior and facilitate market-based economic transactions as well as inclusive institutions that promote political participation. North recognizes that getting the appropriate institutions in place is an uphill struggle since vested interests resist change to preserve the status quo they benefit from. All the authors acknowledge the importance of good leadership.

Once again, while they differ in details, all authors note the importance of path dependence in the evolution of participatory and stable institutions. More specifically, they acknowledge the central role that culture, based on religion and geography, plays in the delivery of these institutions. These institutions evolved first in England and were diffused to nations in the West that shared a similar culture. This does not necessarily undermine the importance of these institutions for social and economic development in low- and middle-income countries (L/MICs), but since most of these nations are culturally different, their path to inclusive institutions is likely to differ.

DOI: 10.4324/9781032630878-6

A more important gap in the NIE development economics narrative is that it implicitly assumes ethnic homogeneity, and that is certainly not the case for constructed nations. In constructed nations rife with poverty, political entrepreneurs have a critical social cleavage to exploit, and hence, they exacerbate political instability and thereby undermine social and economic development. The association of ethnic diversity and conflict is established empirically and also based on a literature review in Chapter 3. Also, the negative association of ethnic diversity and social and economic progress is established in Chapter 3 based on an extensive literature review.

Even low-income natural nations are more willing to invest in inclusive institutions since the beneficiaries are more likely to be "people like us" rather than "the other". As argued in Chapters 2 and 4, such natural nations appear to act in a unified way as though there is a "collective will" to develop.

In Chapter 4, the hypothesis that ethnic homogeneity of a natural nation is likely to be associated with social and economic progress is explored. In fact, a comparative analysis of Bangladesh and Pakistan presents itself as a near-natural experiment to empirically explore this hypothesis, within a conceptual framework of the collective will to act in natural nations presented in Chapter 2. Bangladesh and Pakistan were two provinces (East and West Pakistan) of one country until 1971 when Bangladesh declared its independence after a liberation struggle. Bangladesh has one dominant ethnicity (98 percent Bengalis), whereas Pakistan has six notable ethnic groups. Bangladesh defied all expectations that it would remain a basket case. At the time of its independence in 1971, East Pakistan (now Bangladesh) lagged far behind West Pakistan (now Pakistan) in all social and economic indicators. Five decades later, it far exceeded Pakistan in all social and economic indicators.

It is likely that independence, per se, boosted social and economic performance in Bangladesh, and this hypothesis is also tested in Chapter 4 using the case of Balkan nations that declared independence from the Soviet Union mostly in the early 1990s and in a few cases in the 2000s. Only about half the newly independent Balkan countries could be considered natural nations. In all cases, social and economic progress was dramatic after independence, thereby suggesting that the later status change also plays an important role in boosting a nation's performance.

Most L/LMICs are constructed nations due to their colonial history. While departing, colonial powers hastily determined borders of nations and paid little regard to ethnic integrity and hence doomed them to ongoing ethnic strife into the future. As noted earlier, natural nations have an in-built advantage in attaining national cohesion and hence catch-up growth. Nations not thus blessed have to overcome the disadvantage of ethnic strife by adopting various proven policies to attain national cohesion. These include inclusive political and social policies explored at some length in Chapter 5.

To sum up, the key policy implication of this book for constructed L/LMICs is that they need to first invest in institutions that address horizontal (across ethnicities) inequities that may result from ethnic fractionalization. The premise here is that a prime cause or trigger for catch-up growth is national cohesion and that addressing horizontal inequities, and subsequently vertical inequities (across classes), that create a sense of social justice in the population will harness the productive potential of the bulk of the population.

While the starting point for good leaders in L/LMICs to attain national cohesion is horizontal equity, ignoring vertical equity is risky even for high-income countries (HICs) with evolved institutions. Such inequity also presents political entrepreneurs with a cleavage to exploit as was done by Donald Trump to win the 2016 election in the United States. While evolved institutions can constrain the harm done by cynical exploitation of social cleavages, politics can become dysfunctional even in HICs. Thus, the policy lesson is that sustainable national cohesion can only be built on a broad-based foundation of social justice, including both horizontal and vertical equities.

Index

Note: Page numbers in **bold** indicate a table on the corresponding page.

For Product Safety Concerns and Information please contact our EU
representative GPSR@taylorandfrancis.com
Taylor & Francis Verlag GmbH, Kaufingerstraße 24, 80331 München, Germany